HAPPY CLOUD

EXPLOITATION NATION

Exploitation Nation is published by
Happy Cloud Media, LLC
Vol. 1, No. 10 © 2020

Amy Lynn Best:
Publisher
Mike Watt:
Editor
Carolyn Haushalter:
Asst. Editor
Ally Melling:
Copy Editor

Contributors:
Dr. Rhonda Baughman
Carmine Capobianco
Mike Haushalter
Jason Lane
Michael Legge
Andrew J. Rausch
Terry Thome
Douglas Waltz
Bill Watt
Justin Wingenfeld

Cover art:
Phillip R. Rogers

Art Direction:
Ryan Hose

Special Thanks to:
Allan Arkush
Gorman Bechard
Patrick Casey
Jason Paul Collum
Josh Miller
Frank Henenlotter

Exploitation Nation is published periodically by Happy Cloud Media,
LLC, (Amy Lynn Best and Mike Watt, PO Box 216, Venetia, PA 15617).
Exploitation Nation Issue #10 (ISBN 978-1-951036-20-1) is copyright
2020 by Happy Cloud Media LLC. All rights reserved. All featured
articles and illustrations are copyright 2020 by their respective writers
and artists. Reproductions of any material in whole or in part without
its creator's written permission is strictly forbidden. Exploitation Nation
accepts no responsibility for unsolicited manuscripts, DVDs, stills, art,
or any other materials. Contributions are accepted on an invitational
basis only. **Visit Us At Facebook.Com/ExploitationNation and
www.happycloudpublishing.com**

"You can't tell that joke anymore."

That's what the cops told Lenny Bruce when they arrested him for obscenity in 1961. He used the word "cocksucker" on stage at the Jazz Workshop in San Francisco and then made a couple of linguistic jokes about the phrase "to come" that the authorities found objectionable. That's what our overseers were saying: "Come with us, Mr. Bruce. You can't tell that joke anymore."

I have heard a lot of people using that phrase as a complaint lately, particularly comedians who came into the public eye in the '90s—both a high point and a turning point in comedy. It was a period when observational humor finally supplanted schtick, riding high off the groundbreakers of the late '70s. In the '90s, freedom of speech meant the jaded, educated comedian snarking down the man. "You can't tell that joke anymore," they say, pointing to "PC culture" and "cancel culture," saying, "Young people today can't take a joke." And that's no truer now than it ever was. But right now, even that is beside the point.

It's not the same argument.

It wasn't the audience censoring Bruce, it was the authorities. Sometimes, authority was the butt of Bruce's jokes, but most of his spiel was aimed at hypocrisy. (His book, *How to Talk Dirty and Influence People*, is founded on the concept that people hate each other for their similarities, not their differences, hence his multiple comparisons: "Ray Charles is Jewish. Al Jolson is goyish." It isn't religion, it's essence.) Bruce was an honest crook, and honest crooks use honest words. So, he said "fuck" onstage, and the audience dug what he was saying and how he said it. The pearl-clutchers did what they did best and recoiled in shock. And if he were to be honest (which he was), Bruce would have copped to the shock being at least half of the reason he used the word in the first place.

When Paul Krassner, publisher of *The Realist* and one of the founders of the Yippie movement, printed up signs reading "FUCK COMMUNISM," it spun the mainstream squares into a tizzy. For them, no other words were as foul, as blasphemous as these two, and seeing those words together, expressing a thought they could not say in public, using the dirty word of the underclasses to condemn what

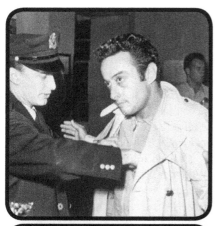

they saw was evil…made them crazy.

Comedy has a lot of magic to it in a linguistic sense. Comedy diffuses taboo first through shock and then by dialogue. The best comedians riff off the shock. "Were you there the night that guy said 'shit'?" asked Albert Brooks in one of his more famous routines. "That was great!" The profane word was what got the attention. Only then can the joke spin out conversation.

"Why is 'fuck' a dirty word?" they've asked. And once the laughter from the shock dies down, the punchline gains the automatic forgiveness of contextual understanding. "It describes something beautiful, something we all want. Why not censor the word 'chocolate'? Or the term 'autoerotic asphyxiation'?"

The ad absurdum just caps the shock. The conversation is always in the middle. And once the conversation is insidiously incepted, dialogue begins. Bruce and Carlin—the *second-*

most-frequently invoked name in the "you can't tell that joke" lament— discussed profanity in culture and thus partially normalized the language. This discussion eased the path ahead for other comedians, including Eddie Murphy, who pushed the dialogue further and in (He would be the first to admit) often ugly ways, because the most successful comedians bring all of their most painful baggage with them onstage and will deny that they are prop comics.

After a while, however, the dialogue overtakes the joke. Because the audience changes. This always happens. It always will happen.

The most wizened of us sometimes haul *Amos 'n' Andy* out of mothballs, lining the pair up alongside Stymie and Buckwheat from the *Our Gang* cast as examples of minstrel. The former is a particularly good example. As a radio show (that ran from 1928 to 1960!), *Amos 'n' Andy* was created and voiced by white actors portraying black characters. The show was set in Harlem, New York, and few of the characters could be seen as upstanding examples of black culture, though they often retained their dignity. In '51, the show moved to television, and black actors moved into the roles at a time when black actors were a scarcity on any screen, much less a medium rapidly jeopardizing movie theater attendance. It made stars out of titular actors Alvin Childress and Spencer Williams. However, the cast still wasn't welcome to sit with white patrons in many public places throughout the country, even among those who enjoyed the show. But the dialogue was starting. Humor got some who

3

hadn't otherwise start asking, "Why can't they?"

That starts, as always, with the audience. And the audience always tells the club owner whom it loves and whom to book. With comedy in particular, the audience is in charge, and, unsurprisingly, the audience comprises a pretty decent cross-section of cultures. Because, while comedy is always subjective, it has wide bands of crossover.

Now, the conversation that started with *Amos 'n' Andy* has long surpassed the presentation. The radio show was clear minstrel, regardless of intention—we are long past intention—and the TV series had problematic elements, mostly stemming from Andy's gambling and laziness. Stereotypes, as always. No longer subtly asking the newly waking audience, "Is this true?" We don't need to ask that question anymore. The answer is "No, goddamn it. Next fucking question."

Because of the questions raised in *Amos 'n' Andy*, we got the rowdier response in *Blazing Saddles*, a Western parody written by an "angry black man" and an anarchistic Jew. It was the intention of Richard Pryor and Mel Brooks to explore the Western through the point of view of a highly intelligent black slave (played by the marvelous Cleavon Little) who accidentally becomes the sheriff of a backwater town. The gag isn't that the slave is intelligent. Save for Gene Wilder's alcoholic gunslinger, the slaves are more intelligent than *everybody else*. The gag is that a bunch of casual white racists suddenly have to rely on a guy they looked down on to save their asses from the obvious villains: the *rich* white guys. They have to confront their prejudices in order to get shit done and work as a community.

Now, I feel that Brooks fumbles the ball with the last act and that the suddenly homophobic dance number is the climax but—in direct contrast to the previous two-thirds—has nothing to say.Another low point is the campfire scene involving beans and excessive flatulence. But I'm in the minority.

Blazing Saddles also gets dinged for the frequent use of the n-word. Pryor had often intoned that the word belonged to the people it was used against. The power belonged to them, not the racists who wielded it as a supposed weapon. In *Blazing Saddles*, the insult stops having a meaning once Black Bart (his name is *Black* Bart! Get it?! *Get it?*) establishes himself as the capable human being in Rock Ridge. The insult becomes meaningless. It's too small to take notice because the speaker is inconsequential. The dialogue is occurs first as a shock and then as a conversation, subtly, under the text (the subtext, if you will).

That was a conversation had at the time it needed to be had. "You can't tell that joke anymore!" Because we no longer have to. What are you mourning? Nobody is taking *Blazing Saddles* away. "But what about *Gone with the Wind*?"

Well, as hilarious as *Gone with the Wind* is, here's something even funnier: Nobody canceled *Gone with the Motherfucking-goddamned-overly-long-fuck-that-movie Wind*. HBOMAX manufactured some mock outrage to further excite the no one who was excited about HBOMAX. HBOMAX hadn't even announced its film library before screaming, "Don't worry! We know all about *Gone with the Wind* and we're doing something about it!"

Suddenly, 10 bazillion people who'd never even seen *Gone with the Wind* suddenly felt outrage over... something...having to do with *Gone with the Wind*. "They're cancelling *Gone with the Wind* !" "They *should* cancel it!" "It's racist!" "It's historical!" "It's too fucking long, and yeah, people are super racist in it, and yeah, they were in the period they were portraying!"

And most of us are over here going, "Who the hell was even *thinking* about *Gone with the Oh-my-god-is-this-still-ON Wind*?" Nobody was until HBOMAX waved its magic controversy wand after making the shocking discovery that the entire world is on its last nerve and blasting air horns at us while we're in lotus pose is just a fucking dick move, HBOMAX. Because unlike comedy, it didn't advance the conversation. It just heckled the headliner.

Nobody 'canceled' *Gone with the Wind* for the same reason that a dwindling amount of people today remember when *Amos 'n' Andy* first started. That audience is vanishing. A new audience is replacing it.

The current audience—the one that may have come of age in the wake of *Blazing Saddles, Amos 'n' Andy*, and even *Richard Pryor: Live on the Sunset Strip*—has decided that those conversations need to be advanced further. Those jokes were told. The spotlight was shone on the exact location the shock took place. Now the conversation has to be less about the n-word and more about the aggression behind it.

Audiences are telling the club owners (and the college campuses and local charities) who is and who is not advancing the conversation. Milo Yoyomasturbator or whoever is not advancing the conversation. He's not welcome at the table because he brings nothing to the potluck that is our collective cultural upheaval. He's just sawing the legs off the chairs.

"You can't tell that joke anymore." Well, you know what other joke you can't tell anymore? Carlin's "Seven Words You Can Never Say on Television" routine. You can't do that bit, not all the way through. *Shit. Piss. Fuck. Cunt. Cocksucker. Motherfucker.* And *Tits.* Maybe they're not in common rotation on *The Big Bang Theory*, but we don't really watch 'television' much anymore, do we? Who watches TV on broadcast? Most of us—the audience members—binge and stream and, I don't know, fuckin' TikTok and shit. And I don't know about you, but I get a steady diet of all seven. "Tits," maybe not so much. I'm told feminists cancelled it.

"Cancelled it." The synonymous phrase in satire for "cancelled it" is "punching down." It's not as much fun. Truly transgressive and memorable comedy waves its private parts at authority. It rallies the new audience to battle. There is always a new authority to skewer. "Punching down" is beneath us. It's why the slaves aren't murdered in *Blazing Saddles*. We already know who really had the power in pre-Civil War America. Two hours of "Ha ha, your entire family is owned like property" isn't funny. "The slave who tamed the West" *is*.

And now, it's time to put to rest that particular conversation and go further. Because the Klan members, while still as stupid as they were in *Blazing Saddles* ("Where the white women at?"—*You can't tell that joke!*"), have crawled back out from under their rocks and are marching around again like the conversation never happened. As in the '60s, comedy may no longer be enough.

Just because the Klan forgot about the conversation doesn't mean we're obliged to catch them back up. It's not our fault that they came in the middle, just so long as they catch the end: They are not welcome.

For the record, you couldn't make *The Producers* today (nor should the film version of the Broadway musical have been made, but that's another argument—i.e., "comedy is subjective"). It was ill-advised in 1967. World War II was still a fresh wound, only 20 years healed. Six million people had been eliminated, not even counting the lives lost on battlefields. Nazis were still a sore subject. Brooks's point was that the titular characters, Max Bialystock (Zero Mostel) and Leo Bloom (Gene Wilder), were betting that audiences would find Nazis beyond the pale. It was only by accident that the offensive play turned out to be funny. Bialystock and Bloom were betting that anti-anti-Semitism would destroy the show. Unfortunately for them, the absurdity won over the atrocity. *The Producers* wasn't mocking anti-Semitism, obviously; it was saying that Nazis were so over-the-top ludicrous in their hate that there was nothing to be afraid of anymore. Nazis were a thing of the past. And yet….

In a 1978 *Maclean's* interview, Brooks said, "More than anything, the great holocaust by the Nazis is probably the great outrage of the 20th century. There is nothing to compare with it. And…so what can I do about it? If I get on the soapbox and wax eloquently, it'll be blown away in the wind, but if I do 'Springtime for Hitler,' it'll never be forgotten. I think you can bring down totalitarian governments

faster by using ridicule than you can with invective."

Today, Nazis are still a sore subject because the Large Hadron Collider brought them back.

No, wait, that's stupid. The ultimate, very unfunny tragedy that is so very close to comedy is that the impeached president in the White House skipped the conversation where we agreed that Nazis were bad. He ain't even *in* the fucking audience. Neither are the Nazis, which is the shit of it and ruins every great Nazi gag ever thought up.

'Nazis are bad' isn't a conversation we should still be having right now, and it's not really funny anymore. My apologies to Matt Stone and Trey Parker, who posited that "everything is funny or nothing is." While, in a perfect world, that would be true, "everything" includes too much punching down. And if too many people skip the conversations, the joke stops being funny. It becomes either mocking or preaching. "You can't tell that joke anymore." Because it stopped being a joke.

Time and place. Perhaps that's the corollary to the Stone/Parker theorem. Or maybe it's the old vaudeville axiom: 'read the room,' a subset of 'know your audience.'

Every racist joke starts with the teller looking over his shoulder.

"I can't tell this joke in mixed company," goes the old gag. "So, would the gentlemen please leave?"

Seinfeld and the "You can't tell that joke" anti-PC this or that or whatever folks—they aren't reading the room. Their audience left during the changeover. It happens. Shows move on and the asses in the seats belong to new owners. The drink minimum varies by state and municipality.

"You can't tell that joke anymore." So, tell a new one.

7

"DYING IS EASY..."
A NOTE ABOUT THE COVER

BY MIKE WATT

In his seminal book *A Glossary of Obscure Words and Phrases in the Writings of Shakespeare and His Contemporaries Traced Etymologically to the Ancient Language of the British People as Spoken Before the Irruption of the Danes and Saxons* (a staple from 1887 in every household library), Charles Mackay notes that the Bard only made use of the term "buskin" once, in *A Midsummer Night's Dream*, and not in a particularly memorable line.

You see, the "sock and buskin" are, by Greek theatrical tradition, two ancient symbols of comedy and tragedy. In Greek theatre, actors in tragic roles wore a boot called a buskin, while comedic actors wore only the *soccus,* or a thin-soled shoe they called, because why not, "a sock."

Sorry, but "boot" and "sock" are poor substitutes for the Greek muses. Melpomene, the muse of tragedy, is sometimes depicted as wearing buskins (or so Wikipedia tells me), whereas the muse of comedy, Thalia, "is similarly associated with the mask of comedy and comic's socks."

"Some people," concludes Wikipedia, "refer to the masks themselves as 'Sock and Buskin.'" However, it fails to identify who these "people" might be so that we can properly avoid them.

Anyway, my point is that our awesome cover began as the sketch below, and Phillip R. Rogers turned it into magic.

COMEDY IS HARD

BY CARMINE CAPOBIANCO

Actually, comedy could be hard. One of the hard parts of comedy is knowing your audience.

And having energy.

When I was in high school and college, I loved *National Lampoon* magazine. They knew their audience. They knew me. They were totally irreverent and showed me boobies. (I even ended up doing a few movies with one of their "boobie girls.") They would never get away with a lot of their stuff today on college campuses. College kids are so PC. You won't find Bluto from *Animal House* on any campus, and you also won't find many stand-up comedians there either. They refuse to go.

Growing up, I collected vinyl albums of stand-up greats like Cosby, the Smothers Brothers, Lenny Bruce, George Carlin, and Woody Allen. I watched the pros on Ed Sullivan, including Stiller and Meara, Shelley Berman, Milton Berle, Alan King, and many more. I was enthralled by *The Honeymooners*, *Andy Griffith*, and *Dick Van Dyke*, and, of course, I loved Lucy. Quite often, we would go to the drive-in and watch the "new" crop of funny people, such as the solo Jerry Lewis, Peter Sellers, and pretty much

the whole cast of *It's a Mad, Mad, Mad, Mad World* doing their own thing. At home, though, is where I cut my teeth on the real funnymen: Abbott and Costello, the Three Stooges, Laurel and Hardy, and the occasional Marx Brothers movie. I must also point out that I was a huge horror fan.

I want to take a second to talk about *Abbott and Costello Meet*

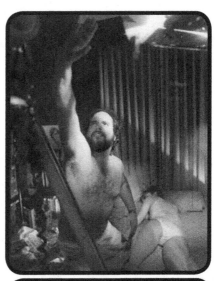

Carmine Capobianco (with Debi Thibault, lounging) filming the incomparable Psychos in Love. (All photos by Kathy Milani / ©PsychosInLove.com. Courtesy of Gorman Bechard)

Frankenstein. What made this an almost perfect comedy was the fact that the monsters played it straight. Bud and Lou played themselves, but Frankenstein's monster (Frankenstein himself never appeared), the Wolfman, and Dracula were the horror icons we grew to love. The scene where Lou sits on Frankenstein's monster's lap was, to me, as a kid, frightening and funny at the same time. It brought my two favorite genres together, and as an 11-year-old, I considered it my go-to movie anytime it was televised (no VCRs yet). The problem I have with the movie now is—like the movies after it where Abbott and Costello meet the Mummy, Dr. Jekyll and Mr. Hyde, and the Invisible Man—there weren't any classic routines. Now I have the Blu-ray and my son and I will watch it every once in a while. Afterward, we go to YouTube and watch some version of their *Who's on First?* routine. Now, we watch and

laugh at the Mel Brooks/Gene Wilder masterpiece *Young Frankenstein.* But that's a whole other 4,000-word essay. I think it's time to show my son *Monty Python and the Holy Grail.*

In the early '70s, I was in Waldenbooks, pulled Richard Anobile's *Why a Duck? Visual and Verbal Gems from the Marx Brothers Movies* off a shelf and started to thumb through it. The book consisted of frame-by-frame blow-ups of scenes from several Marx Brothers movies, complete with the actual dialogue from the films. It was on sale and I bought it.

The book changed my views on comedy. I still loved everyone I mentioned before, but I became obsessed with these guys—especially the unreleased gem *Animal Crackers* with Anobile's *Hooray for Captain Spaulding: Verbal & Visual Gems from "Animal Crackers."* Then, in 1974, *Animal Crackers* was finally rereleased in theaters after remaining unseen for decades. It immediately became my favorite film of all time (and still is to this day). Seeing it performed live at the Goodspeed Opera House in East Haddam, Conn., was a huge thrill, and meeting the entire cast was a fun event. I spoke to the actor who became famous for playing Groucho for years, Frank Ferrante, and questioned him on a missing scene. His mouth dropped and he asked me how I noticed that. My mouth dropped when he told me that they edited out some of the scenes and musical numbers because they felt today's audiences would not sit for that length of time. I would have sat longer and then watched it again.

In 1975, another life-changing

Cast co-operation is always appreciated.

Most couples continued to dance, but those who listened to the words stopped and laughed through the song. When it was over, those who stopped dancing reacted with loud applause and whistles, while others were confused about what was happening.

This song reinforced what the Marxes and Pythons were showing me: You don't need to put on a red nose to reinforce that you are doing comedy. The realness of the situations, coupled with lines spoken seriously that add to the absurdity, will get you a laugh every time.

Good comedy has targets. It may shock a race, a nationality, or even a gender. It may make the villain look like a buffoon, or it may simply be self-deprecating. It may point out what is obvious to us, or, in its blatancy, a punch line may fool us by *not* surprising us. There's the running joke that may or may not be funny the first time, but the more we hear it, the harder we laugh. With some comedians or movie dialogue, it is the storytelling that resonates in our memories, and we laugh at the ridiculousness of situations through which we lived. Let's not also forget about a good double entendre and bad puns.

As I get older, I find that comedians who resort to jokes about sex and their body parts are not funny. Excessive cursing no longer makes me laugh out loud (Sorry, Richard and George), and political comedians who use insults to further their agendas

movie was released: *Monty Python and the Holy Grail.* This and *Animal Crackers*, especially, taught me so much about comedy. A year later, during my senior year in high school, I was allowed to do several solo performances in the school variety show in front of the curtain as scenery was being changed behind it. When I heard the live audience laugh and saw that on several nights, I received standing ovations, I fell in love with making people laugh. I knew that it was quite possible that I could become a funnyman.

Before the band that I was in changed from a party band to a wedding band (which I couldn't stand and quit), I was allowed to work the crowd. The laughter I heard made me happy. I had written a beautiful ballad and introduced it as such and began to play the lovely opening piano part. The young couples stood up and began to slow dance in front of us, and I began to sing. The words were about a man who just didn't like his girlfriend anymore, and the song was full of insults. It was titled "I Hate You." We always got a similar reaction.

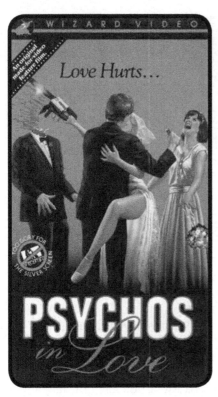

how many people have actually seen it. I played Detective Joe Tremaglio (a name I used in every subsequent movie I made with director Gorman Bechard—except *Galactic Gigolo*, in which we spelled the name backwards and I was "Eoj Oilgamert").

I wasn't really an actor, so Gorman let me just play myself and ad-lib most everything. It worked, and viewers liked the character who was, at times, the comic relief, but by playing it straight in absurd situations.

We tried our hand at drama by cowriting a piece of crap called *And Then?* which never saw the light of day except on a local cable station. The director of the station took a chance and aired this even though it had adult language and nudity. Through some video-based black hole, I was awarded an award for best supporting actor.

We now realized that it was drama that was hard and began cowriting *Psychos in Love*, a horror film/romantic comedy that takes place in a universe where murderers never get caught. The murders were serious, many of the characters were serious, and the romance was real. The script was funny, and whenever Gorman sent me scenes to rewrite, I pushed them over the edges of the proverbial envelope. Sometimes, but not always, Gorman would bring it back just to the edge.

Casting was done perfectly, and during the shoot, there were plenty of questions. Every person, save one, understood what we were going for, and filming was not only easy (even though there were a few days over 24 hours), it was pure joy. Scenes were changed, shortened, lengthened, and

bore me or tick me off (too easy for 50 percent of their audiences). I don't like comedians who are just mean—I mean *really* mean. Comedy is supposed to make you smile or laugh and not shake your head and say, "Those poor bastards." Yes, yes, I know that there are targets in a lot of comedy, but there's no need to bring a Luger to a butter knife fight.

This brings me to how I got to be known as a funny guy around the world (not by everybody around the world, but a few people in a lot of countries). (I still blush when certain fans refer to me as a "comedic genius," but that's worth blushing for.)

The first feature film I appeared in was a little ditty known as *Disconnected*. Although not a huge commercial success, I am amazed at

at one point, we wrote a scene on set. And there was ad-libbing. This was mostly by me since I can't remember lines exactly. However, the best part was the laughing. Everybody laughed, and most everyone fell in love with each other and became life-long friends.

The movie was sold to what is now Full Moon, and we were offered a 35mm four-movie deal. Gorman and I tried to recreate the magic of *Psychos in Love* with a script that had an even sillier premise: *Galactic Gigolo*. This story was that a broccoli from a planet inhabited by walking, talking vegetables wins a trip to a small town on Earth known as the horniest place in the galaxy. So, the horror/romantic comedy becomes a sci-f/kind of romantic comedy, which we attempted to film like a cartoon. We used brightly colored gels to alter the lighting, but when we sent the film to post-production at Full Moon, they corrected (and destroyed) the colors. Their editing was not what it should have been, the music was goofy, and it didn't look like we were having fun making it. Some of the performances were way over the top, and sometimes, they screamed, "Hey! I'm being funny over here!" The most embarrassing part of the movie was the climax. The editors had no idea about comedy, and there was no rhythm or pacing. I truly believe if we had control of post-production, the movie would have been a lot more entertaining. Why? Because we understood what we were trying to do, and we knew what worked before.

So, I now know that to some people, comedy is hard.

Nothing (or nobody) can be funnier than a seasoned stand-up comedian. Why? Because he or she recites the material over and over again, and a bright comedian will listen to what gets the laughs and what doesn't. If it is something he thinks is funny and barely anyone chuckles, he may try to reword it, rework it, and reorganize it before his next show and then listen to the audience's reaction again. He

"Look over there!" "Where?" Debi as Kate, Carmine as Joe, Frank Stewart as Herman. (Caption recycled from Movie Outlaw: The Prequel, by Mike Watt. Cuz it's FUNNY!)

13

continues to tweak it until he gets what he wants from his audience. If no matter what he does the joke falls flat, he drops it. It's history.

The Marx Brothers took on the road many of the potential "skits" they had written for their movies. They would perform these before live audiences. They listened to what worked best and then preserved it exactly, locking it in for the film. They rarely ad-libbed.

According to Charlotte Chandler in her book *Hello, I Must Be Going: Groucho and His Friends,* in her interview with Robert Pirosh (a contributor to the dialogue in *A Night at the Opera* and *A Day at the Races*), Groucho "was a perfectionist in his work. On this road tour, on the *Night at the Opera* road tour, we'd have a scene down pat, and he would know, everyone would know where the laugh comes and about how long it's going to last, how long a pause to take. He'd try every possible thing, and sometimes, by switching one word around or by using another word, he would get a laugh."

Pirosh goes into a bit more detail. "I remember one line. Harpo was playing a harp, and Groucho kept heckling him. S. A. Schearer was a well-known name then. They were pawnbrokers and they advertised a lot. So, one of his lines while he's heckling Harpo was, 'There's a man outside. He's from S. A. Schearer. He's here to get the harp.' It got a laugh. Then, the next time he came in, it would be different. 'S. A. Schearer is here for the harp.' And the next time, it would be, 'S. A. Schearer sent a man here for the harp.' You know, he'd keep trying everything, and one of them

would get a bigger laugh than the others. Nobody knows why, but he'd stick to that."

I know why and now you know why.

We filmed *Psychos in Love* on 16mm short ends, which are partial rolls of unexposed film stock left over from another shoot and sold to a film dealer, who would resell it back to us. It was a cheaper way to go since full rolls of 16mm film were quite expensive. Plus, we had to develop the film and get a work print for viewing and editing. Then, the negative was edited, and the final film was printed from that. Today, everything is digital, and the cost of film, which can run into tens of thousands of dollars on a low-budget film, is wiped out of the final cost.

We needed to save money whenever we could. We rarely filmed a scene more than once, and there were no "outtakes" for a blooper reel. The solution was to rehearse each scene over and over until we felt we got it right. The main rule on this film was that once the film is running, you better damn well have everything perfect. But this was a comedy, and the over-rehearsing was like taking the sketches on the road. At first, I worried that rehearsing so much would make everything stale, but it had the opposite effect for a lot of us. We rehearsed, and Gorman—a pretty funny guy his own damn self—would make a suggestion for the dialogue or the action. We listened to the room and waited for the laughs or the silence. We tried it again and I tried something else. Again, we listened to the room. By the time the camera started rolling those short ends, we had a pretty tight scene. And a damn funny one.

For most of us, the perfect example was the scene where Joe is behind the bar and Kate comes running in excitedly to tell Joe something. She is constantly interrupted by the Chinese man in the Karate uniform, who orders a beer by just saying the word "one." Right after he does that, though, either Kate or I ask a question. Lum Chang Pang, who played that part, was from Brooklyn and had a heavy accent. When he answered one of the questions that wasn't meant for him with "Cuz I'm thuh-stee" and a totally deadpan face, I would always burst out laughing, causing the room to break. Gorman claims he couldn't get through the scene because my shoes sounded like suction cups on the wet bar mats behind the counter.

We rehearsed over and over again because the scene was all about timing, and we hoped that the literal tears of laughter would subside because we were getting used to Lum's straight-faced delivery. We were filming in a real strip club, so we couldn't start any production until the bar closed. The time was going fast. At about 4:30 in the morning, Gorman called that we were going to film this scene. We all kind of stiffened and reluctantly agreed. When you watch the movie, you will notice that my character is having a tough time holding it together. When Gorman said "cut," there was a huge round of applause and lots of laughter and hugs. We had shot my second-favorite scene in the movie. To me, it is still the funniest because I was there and we found the funniest way to do the scene.

By the way, my favorite scene in the movie is the very last. I am a firm believer in the audience always leaving the theater feeling the final scene. The last scene in our movie is funny and sweet and sums up the beautiful relationship the two serial killers had during the course of the movie.

Before I had my son, seventeen years after my third daughter, I really wanted to introduce my three lovely ladies to the "old-time comedians." I owned a few video stores and thought I would try a little experiment after I wore a Marx Brothers tie one day and a teenager asked me which presidents were on my tie. I told him they were the Marx Brothers, and after a long, frustrating conversation, the only way he remotely knew them was through the Vlasic Pickles stork. I then got excited when he asked me if I had any old movies, so I took him to the "Classics" section. He told me he hated black and white and by "old," he meant from the '80s. Something is wrong here, and I will be ding-dang damned if my daughters even remotely turn out like this nimrod.

I grabbed a VHS tape (DVDs weren't around yet) of *Abbott and Costello Meet Jerry Seinfeld* and brought it home, pulling a "gather 'round, girls." They reluctantly lined up on the couch, I quickly explained who Bud and Lou were, and we watched. Before the *Who's on First?* routine came on, I thought I should explain it and have a little fun with my little girls. I did this with my son years later.

"OK, listen. There are three bases, right? On first base is a guy named Who. That's his name. Second base had a guy named What, and third base had a guy named I Don't Know." They looked a little confused, so I explained it again. Then, I quizzed them. "Tell me the name of the guy on first base."

"Who!" they squealed.

"The guy on first base," I teased.

"Who!" they started to laugh. And they understood and learned another facet of comedy.

The magic of the boys worked, and my girls were soon laughing out loud. These were their best routines, and they probably were going to be hard to follow.

A few days later, I called the girls from the store and read them the list of Abbott and Costello movies I could bring home. For some odd reason, they chose *Abbott and Costello Meet the Invisible Man*. I would have chosen *Buck Privates* or *Abbott and Costello Meet Frankenstein*, but I was still trying to get my foot in the door. They loved it.

They weren't too fond of the Stooges or Laurel and Hardy but totally fell in love with Harpo Marx. That was completely understandable. Harpo was a mischievous imp and very childlike. They loved the scene in *Duck Soup* that ends with Harpo splashing his feet around in Edgar Kennedy's vat of lemonade.

It dawned on me what children love. They love to see other kids, like Harpo, getting one over on the adults (see *Home Alone*). They also love to be in on a joke, like in *Who's on First?* And they love to be teased by an adult deliberately playing dumb.

Teenagers are a tough call. In my video store, I offered them free rentals to expose to them some of these old comedians. Many took me up on the offer, especially at the encouragement of their parents. Many ended up being "too cool for school" and came back shaking their

Debi Thibault and corpse in repose.

heads. Sometimes, if they returned the movie without their parents around, they said they thought it was funny or said it was stupid. I couldn't tell if they were being truthful or not. Then, they rented *Ace Ventura* and left.

I'm not sure who our exact target audience was for *Psychos in Love*, but if I were to guess, it would be a guy in his twenties who loved slasher films and boobs. But then we had the romance, so maybe a few women too. But then we had references and/or a homage or two to classic comedians (Groucho's "She's either dead or my watch has stopped" or the Abbott and Costello-inspired wedding scene), and we satirized the persona of Michael Myers with a screaming exotic dancer who would not die. So, maybe our target audience was someone older. I'm all over the board with my guesses.

My youngest daughter sent me a text when she was in her late teens that simply said, "You're a genius." When I asked her why, she texted back that she just watched the movie and loved it. During the pandemic, my oldest daughter, who is 32, texted me that her husband wanted to watch the movie again that particular night. My middle daughter, an amazing actress, doesn't like the movie. In a few years, I'll show it to my son.

When the Internet, especially Facebook, became prevalent, we found out that there were fans of all ages all over the world. Some of these fans remembered the dialogue better than we did. *Psychos in Love* was loved by this wonderful cross section around the globe. Meeting these fans at conventions always means so much to me.

So, seriously, really, is comedy hard? It's hard if you don't understand it. It's hard if you don't know why or to whom you're trying to be funny. It's hard if you don't take it seriously. It's hard if you don't know how to react. It's hard if you don't know how to get that twinkle in your eye. It's hard if you don't know when to pull back. It's hard if you're not familiar with how to manipulate the language. It's hard if you are always PC. It's hard if you are afraid of being ridiculous. It's hard if you are afraid to "be on" and let your weird little mind always turn.

Comedy is exhausting. The only thing you have to be careful of is ending up being predictable. There are two kinds of predictable. One type of predictable is when your audience knows what your punchline will be in some way, shape, or form. This is the worst. The second type of predictable is when your audience knows that you *will* make a funny comment in the next moment. That one's not so bad.

I get a lot of eye-rolling from my kids, but my brother will laugh hysterically at the stupid stuff I say. I will immodestly state that I am a good storyteller. So, I have that.

At home, with my girlfriend, I will deliberately say things that are ridiculous. I took her to a couple of screenings, and people have asked her if I am that funny at home. She sighs and says, "Yes." I guess it gets to be too much. But I love hitting my goal at home. That's when I go over the top and she says, without malice, "You're an idiot."

My goal with all of you reading this is a smile or a laugh. That is when I feel like I am king of the world. Thank you for that.

Seriously.

CHEAP LAUGHS
THE TRAGICOMEDY HISTORY
OF SIDESHOW CINEMA

BY MICHAEL LEGGE

The story goes that on his death bed, actor Edmund Gwenn[1] uttered the famous line, "Dying is easy. Comedy is hard." Comedy *is* hard. The hardest comedy to do is to avoid the vulgar, crude, shock tactics to which a lot of modern comedy movies resort. We still haven't gotten over snorting at "naughty words" spoken out loud. It's the cheapest laugh there is. That's why I usually avoid it. As my hero, Groucho Marx, observed, "Anybody can say something dirty and get a laugh. But say something clean and get a laugh—that requires a comedian."

As a fat, nonathletic kid, I was already set apart from most boys. I was a misfit. Then, a miracle occurred: I found I could make people laugh, even adults! I had an early gift for mimicry, and I remember clearly a group of boys gathered around me during recess while I imitated the various cartoon characters that were on TV at that time. It was a strange sort of gift to deal with, but it gained me acceptance.

The television became my teacher for Comedy 101. I got hooked on the Three Stooges, Laurel and Hardy, and, especially, the Marx Brothers. Abbott and Costello entered my world via *Abbott and Costello Meet Frankenstein*.

Once my family bought a home movie camera, I had a new fascination: making up stories to shoot and watch. My giant insect toys became my first stars on film. All of this led me to do short blackout skits on film. I recruited my like-minded friends and we had a ball that first summer, making about 11 short films.

There is nothing more irritating to me than when a legit critic or a sofa snark proclaims that something is not funny. They tend to forget the qualifier "to me." No one has the authority to tell you what is and is not funny.

I've been an actor in live theatre for a few decades, and I can tell you that there's a whole different kind of anxiety bubbling inside you when you're performing a comedy. If you're doing a drama, you want the audience to be quiet, but for a comedy, you want the opposite. You want laughs, or at least chuckles. I can't tell you how deflated an actor gets onstage if

---

1   These were, reportedly, among Gwenn's last words, spoken to his friend, director George Seaton, in 1959. I wasn't there.

the audience is subdued or comatose. It's murder. You want the play to get over with so you can go home. Making a comedy movie is dealing with the unknown. Your movie will be seen in someone's home. They may not pay strict attention. You'll never know what they laugh at (if they laugh at all).

What's your taste? High comedy? Low comedy? Mine is a mixture of both. My films have been predominantly absurd and silly. If anything shows through in my films, it's the love of comedy teams rather than a single comedian supported by straight men and women. I have a proclivity to satire. For me, *Dr. Strangelove* is the greatest satire ever filmed. Other movie satires include *Network*, *Monty Python's Life of Brian*, and *Airplane*. Television in the 1960s served up some notable satires. *Get Smart* skewered the spy genre, portraying our protectors of democracy as incompetent or hypocritical and mocking stereotypes. *F Troop* subversively turned the Western genre on its head. Where you can get into trouble is in your audience misinterpreting your intention. You can mock and show how ridiculous stereotypes are when you're doing satire, sometimes by doing an exaggerated version of it, or sometimes by reversing it. In my movie *Honey Glaze*, I played what appeared to be the typical Asian villain, Dr. Sum Thaim. However, I was purposely mocking the vile stereotype of the "yellow menace." After my short film *Joe X* was screened at a film festival in Ann Arbor, I was cornered by some young women who questioned my portrayals of the women in the film.

Joe X was a film noir/Hitchcock spoof. I was satirizing the idiotic notion presented in some older movies that women like to be treated roughly. They misunderstood my intention. I was showing how ridiculous that was. Thankfully, they did finally see where I was coming from.

In the late '70s, I started making short films that I finally thought were good enough for the public to see. I had some encouragement from various film festivals in Michigan, Toronto, Pennsylvania, and Florida, where I won some awards. My short film *The Lemon Man* was broadcast multiple times on USA Network's show *Night Flight* during the mid-1980s.

Newly armed with a Super 8 sound film camera, I embarked on a feature film, *Working Stiffs*. As a postal worker, I tended to feel like a zombie, working round the clock six days a week. It became the inspiration for the movie. We did the best we could with what we had for resources, and I was able to snag some real locations for the film. My love of horror and comedy is often mixed in my films, and *Working Stiffs* is a prime example. Nothing against George Romero, but I didn't like that cannibalism had become the definition of the zombie. So, I used the original version of a zombie—that of a mindless slave. In the film, I play Don Drago, who runs the hiring agency Con Temps. While vacationing in Haiti, Drago obtains the secret of raising the dead. During job interviews, the applicant is murdered, is raised from the dead, and becomes a mindless temp worker who doesn't need vacations, sick pay, or lunch breaks. The company

From "Working Stiffs," dir. Michael Legge.

pockets the zombie's salary. Despite the fact that Working Stiffs was made for little money, I thought it came out pretty well. Luckily, I had been doing live theatre for years, so I was able to recruit actors who could do the job. The main cast included Bruce Harding, Mike McInnis, Beverly Epstein, Alan Kennedy, and Tony Ferreira.

This was long before the digital age, so distribution had to be done as VHS tapes. I looked for a distributor and found one—a bad one. This guy talked big and delivered nothing. He wanted me to buy ads for the trade magazines, but I had no money. As it was, I had to pay for the VHS copies. It took a while, but I extricated myself from this clown and tried again. I got luckier the second time around. A company named Salt City Cinema (now called Sub Rosa) liked the film. Ron Bonk, the company head, became a big supporter of my films, for which I will always be grateful.

Working Stiffs did do me a favor. The National Endowment for the Arts was doling out grant money to state arts agencies. In Massachusetts, the Boston Film/Video Foundation distributed money to film projects. You had to not only pitch your film project to them, but you also had to submit a complete work. I submitted Working Stiffs. I didn't expect to get anything. I was very surprised when I was awarded a grant for a few thousand dollars to finance my next movie, Loons. I subsequently had one of the judges on the committee tell me that after seeing submissions of documentaries or heavy dramas, it was breath of fresh air to see a movie that was funny and silly.

During this time, I discovered I was sterile. I was the end of the line for my family name. This sparked the Loons premise of a cursed family that wants to die out. Loons was a more elaborate project. There was a big restaurant scene in it, so I had to rent out a function room in a local restaurant and buy enough food for people to be seen eating during the scene. We also lucked out in being able to use a local senior facility for the mental hospital scenes. One pothole we hit in the production was that the original female lead bailed on us after the first day of shooting, and I had to reshoot all her scenes again with a new actor. That was a few hundred dollars down the drain. In the film, Jeff Coukos (Jim O'Brien) brings home his fiancée (Diane Mela) to meet his mother (Linda Baxter Hardy). His mother doesn't want her son to get married and have children. *Loons* involves a witch's curse cast upon the Loon family and all its male descendants. The curse caused the males of the family to go insane once they reach 30 years old. It was a huge cast and a crazy film. It also seems to be a fan favorite among Sideshow Cinema aficionados.

Loons had a rocky period. In the '90s, there were a few magazines devoted to indie films. One of them had an ad for a company named Milestone Productions. They were soliciting indie films for distribution. I submitted *Loons* and it was accepted. Long story short, the guy running it was another do-nothing who started stonewalling not only me, but fellow filmmaker Mark Polonia. We both had to take legal steps to get our materials back.

Loons came out quite well and did me the same favor that *Working Stiffs* did: It got me another grant for my next movie, *Cutthroats*. Again, I was bashing the mindless work ethic and the creeps you're sometimes forced to work for. *Cutthroats* is a nightmare office comedy. Some have noticed a resemblance in some respects to the mainstream production of *Office Space*. However, *Cutthroats* came out before that film.

Most of *Cutthroats* takes place in an office. Again, we were fortunate enough to snag a couple of real locations from a local business. I think that anyone in any workplace could identify with the beleaguered main character, Don Drinkwater (Alan Kennedy), as he tries to just get through each day without getting

A pair of "Loons."

21

backstabbed by one of his fellow workers, namely Roger Digger (James Porter). He also suffers from insomnia, which doesn't help any.

The last movie I shot on film was a short one titled *Sick Time*. It eventually became part of the anthology movie I made, *Night Basement*. I played Rod Surly in my best tight-lipped manner as I introduced three stories, *The Lemon Man* and *Sick Time* (both shot on film), as well as *Stage Blood* (shot on video).

Before I detail my video period, I should explain how difficult it was to shoot on Super 8 sound film. Major movies were shot on negative film, which was processed and then printed onto positive stock. Super 8 was called reversal film: The film you were shooting, when processed, became a positive print. The soundtrack was a thin magnetic stripe on the edge of the film. The camera was hooked up to a microphone for the sound to be recorded live. This was known as single-system sound. When I made a few 16mm films, I used double system. That's when a separate tape recorder was either connected to the camera or was recording a sync signal from the camera. Super 8 cameras didn't have a through-the-lens viewfinder. You had to focus using a ground glass circle in the viewfinder. A good camera had manual exposure, so you could zoom in on the subject, get a light reading, and then lock that setting. However, many times, you would get film back with soft focus or over/underexposed footage because you weren't seeing exactly what the lens was photographing.

Editing had to be done in a clumsy way. Instead of cutting by picture, you had to cut by sound. The soundtrack on a film reel was about a second ahead of the picture, so if you cut by the picture only, you were at risk of chopping off words of dialogue. You had to cut by the dialogue. Not that you couldn't cut for picture only; you could if no live dialogue was involved. You spliced the shots together with a special splicing tape. But the best part of all was that you had to wait two-three weeks to get the film back from the lab. If it was loused up, you had to shoot it all over again. When we were shooting *Loons*, one reel of film never came back from the processor, so we had to shoot the scenes over again. That reel of film showed up in the mail one year later. By this time, I wanted an alternative to film.

Regular VHS was a middling-quality medium, but along came Super VHS, which upped the quality considerably. I invested in a S-VHS camera and bought a very expensive editing suite that consisted of two machines: a playback console and a recorder console. The two were connected to a control board. *Potential Sins* was my first S-VHS movie.

At least now I could have some instant gratification by seeing what we shot right after we shot it. There was no waste. You could rerecord over the tape when necessary. *Potential Sins* is quite a dark comedy, as I was in a dark place mentally during the shooting. It involves a surprise birthday party that backfires when the honored guest tries to kill himself in the upstairs bedroom.

The cast included Phyllis Rittner, Phil Fougere, Steve Mullahoo, Alan Kennedy, and other talented recruits

22

From "Potential Sins."

from the stage. I was diagnosed with clinical depression at the time. I was going through the process of finding which medication would help me. It was not a fun time, and the wrong med can make things worse. I was using the movie as a cathartic release, pretending to kill myself in a movie rather than really doing it. I struggled with medication for a year or so until I found one that kept me stable. No wonder my next film was called *Braindrainer*!

Braindrainer is a sci-fi comedy about a small meteorite that houses an alien intelligence striking Earth. All of the intelligence is drained from anyone who touches the rock. I tried to make this one the ultimate B-movie. I was lucky to have a friend to do some special video effects of the meteor heading toward Earth. I played the Amazing Jacques, a sleazy hypnotist. I based the character on the hypnotist from the movie *The Hypnotic Eye*. Jacques Bergerac, a French actor, played the bad guy in that one, so

for my film, I did a phony accent. We also had the Creeper (Ed Eck) and the Spiderwoman (Michelle Leibowitz) as characters. Although it was a fun film to shoot, I was always disappointed with the technical results. I still wasn't sold on S-VHS for shooting movies, and I tried to get fancy by using gelled lighting, which just made everything look either overexposed or a sickly color. The viewfinder tended to be a little inaccurate as well, and some of the shots wound up slightly out of focus. All in all, I wish I had made the film when we finally ventured into digital. But I had one more video left to make.

Curtains is a fleshed-out version of a short film I made in the 1980s. It involves three spirits stuck in limbo because they didn't believe in an afterlife. In this context, limbo is sitting in the back of pickup truck as it circles a block for eternity. We hear the back stories of the passengers, played by Bruce Adams, Cherry Zinger, and me. I managed to satirize cults, Hitchcock movies, and film noir, but I showed some hope for deliverance at the end.

Then, ta-da! The digital age caught up with me, and boy was I glad to meet it. My first digital movie was titled *Honey Glaze*. I had loved the '60s TV show *Honey West*, starring the gorgeous Anne Francis, so I decided to spoof both the spy and detective genres. In the movie, Honey (Lorna Nogueira) is a child/woman who was so protected by her secret agent father that she never emotionally matured past 10 years old. When her father (Ed Dunn) is murdered, she has to grow up fast to avenge his death. As mentioned earlier, I played Dr. Sum Thaim. Again, this was an obvious

23

"Coffee Run."

takeoff on the Asian villain Dr. No. Thaim is aided by the incredibly inept Nurse Tarika (Cherry Zinger).

Shooting digitally was a whole new world. This time, I could clearly see what I was shooting. Editing on the computer gave me such ease and speed; it was a dream. Now I could shuffle around shots and extend or shorten them without losing valuable footage. I could also insert special effects, which I could never do on Super 8. Best of all, digital filmmaking costs nothing if you own the camera and the editing software. I could never pay my actors on my salary, so I only had to buy props or special clothes for each film.

My movie *Democrazy* was probably my most trashed movie. Our president at the time was George W. Bush. I played a variation of him, and the right-wingers ganged up on social media to attack it. I was actually making fun of both sides and the human race in general, but satire is a mirror, and you might not like what you see. But as someone once said, "There are some people one wishes to offend." We got to use a planetarium in a local college for a major set. That set, coupled with a video demonstrating that Earth is "deflating," added some nice touches to this crazy film.

The digitals came in rapid succession, though they were not all that easy to make. When we were shooting *My Mouth Lies Screaming*, my camera died, and I had to buy a new one to finish the movie. *MMLS* was a takeoff on the giallo genre. The unique way of killing in this one was with a bow tie (No, not a standard bow tie, but the clip-on type). The victims were slashed to death with the sharp end of the little metal clasps. I like to push silliness to an extreme. One of the characters, Dumbelina (Diane Mela), gets her head cut off, but a genius surgeon (played by Phil Hall) sews her head back on, and she's as good as new—well, almost good as new. *MMLS* is one of my all-time favorite movies because everything seemed to fall into place.

Evan Straw was my only deviation from comedy. I was friends with someone at work who lived in this great circa 1700s house. I thought it the perfect place for a ghost story, but

I wanted to make it different. I found a way. Lorna Nogueira played the lead in this one and gave an extraordinary performance. To add to the fun, my fellow horror host Danielle Gelehrter (a.k.a. Penny Dreadful) played a psychic in the movie. As the ghost hunter who figures it all out, I dyed my hair white and wore dark glasses throughout the film.

After a few years of playing Dr. Dreck in my public access program *The Dungeon of Dr. Dreck*, I had grown so fond of the characters that I felt like a movie featuring Dreck and his cohost, Moaner (Lorna Nogueira), would be fun to do. I set it in the '60s and shot it in black and white. The film shows how Dreck and Moaner became TV icons and aroused the ire of the station's prima donna TV host, Louise Morgan. Louise was played by the late Phyllis Weaver, who excelled in playing awful people even though she herself was the sweetest person you'd ever meet. John Shanahan played her milquetoast son, Lester, in another wonderful performance. The movie had a William Castle moment as a movie within the movie played for a few minutes. It required the use of Spook Specs to see the ghosts clearly in that segment. I included a pair of red-lensed glasses in the DVD case.

I love black-and-white movies, so *Monochromia* came next. The story of a scientific experiment gone horribly wrong started out in color. But the plague that settles on mankind is devastating. The fallout affects the eyes and destroys a person's ability to see in color. Naturally, a rich madman pursues the cure so that he can sell it to everyone on Earth and become even more filthy rich. Why? Because, as he says, "I like to pretend it's the first time."

Along the way came *Coffee Run*, another movie that shows the insanity of the human race. *The Brothers Dim*, a twisted fairy tale, was coupled with a Dr. Dreck sequel, *Who Stole Shrunken Ed?*

Planet Void involves an alternate Earth wherein all the males have died out, but the females are getting along just fine without them. An alien with the opposite problem arrives: His race has lost all its females. He offers to help them bring back males if they help him bring back females. But do the women want men back?

A lot of years and tears have gone by since that first film in 1988. I found that making movies was becoming more and more stressful. When you don't pay the actors, you have to conform to their schedules, which is totally understandable. However, I tended to have rather large casts, and getting actors to show up on the same day and at the same time became more and more onerous. I often had to shoot around them, having one actor address another who wasn't there at the time and then repeating the process and cutting the shots together. Although we still had a good time shooting the movies, I felt it had finally worn me down so much that the fun had gone out of it.

My last movie, a sci-fi comedy, was titled *Crawlers*. It sprang out of a nightmarish idea I had one night. I read in bed before sleep, and the door to my room is open to a dark hallway. One night, I thought how creepy it would be if I heard noise in the hall and some person came into my room on their hands and knees: a human nightcrawler. Of course I turned the idea around to make it funny. The "crawlers" are people from the future. They go through a temporal field and land in our time. It gets complicated from there, but overall, I thought I went out on a good, solid comedy.

I wouldn't have come this far without the moral support of several writers and fellow filmmakers, such as Kevin Lindenmuth, Paul Scrabo, Phil Hall, Dwight Kemper, Douglas Waltz, and especially the first people to give me encouragement, Bob Brodsky and Toni Treadway.

Have I given up comedy completely? Not quite. One thing I thought I could do is make animated short films, which wouldn't require juggling peoples lives. My first one is titled *Coffee Hell* and it is currently on Amazon. I just finished my second short, *Fool Bus*. I do the male voices, and Lorna Nogueira supplies the females.

To wrap up with a shameless plug, I've also written a number of books. As Dr. Dreck, I've written *Dr.*

Dreck's B Movie Museum and *Monster Kidding*. *Lurking in the Late Night* is about growing up with late-night TV. *Outlandish Adventures* is a book of wacky short stories, the main one featuring Fussy Eagleton, Secret Busboy. My latest, *Escape from the Domain*[2], is a novella that should also tickle B-movie fanatics. These are all for sale on Amazon and Barnes and Noble (hint hint).

There you have it. Comedy is hard. You can make all of the people laugh some of the time and some of the people laugh all of the time, but you can't make all of the people laugh all of the time. If I did, that would worry me.

Mike's movies can be found here:
https://michaellegge52.wixsite.com/mysite/sideshow-cinema

His Amazon author page is:
https://www.amazon.com/Michael-Legge/e/B001K7LQ64

---

2 This book was reviewed in *Exploitation Nation* #7.

Lorna Nogueira as Moaner Johnson and Michael Legge as Dr. Dreck.

THE ALTERNATE UNIVERSES OF MICHAEL LEGGE

BY DOUGLAS WALTZ

Having actually written a book on Michael Legge (No, really, it's on Amazon and everything), I thought it would be nice to examine his final trilogy of movies. While they don't comprise an actual trilogy, these films do all embrace the theme of "What if...?" Back in the day, Marvel Comics had a long-running series of comics titled *What If?* The series would skew things that were preestablished in the Marvel Universe. "What If Someone Else Besides Spider-Man Had Been Bitten by the Radioactive Spider?", "What If Spider-Man Joined the Fantastic Four?", and "What If the Punisher Had Killed Daredevil?" were among some of the issue titles.

You get the idea.

In his final trilogy of films, Legge explores (in the order reviewed) "What if the entire world were colorblind?", "What if there was a planet inhabited only by women?", and "What if the Hollow Earth theory were fact?"

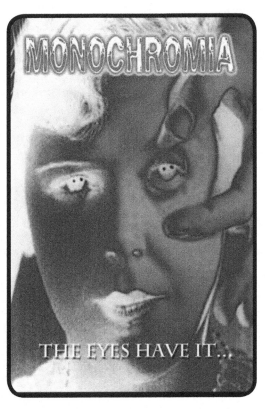

Monochromia. This film depicts a world in which a scientist who designs chemical warfare weapons creates a new gas called Checkerboard. The gas effectively makes whoever is in the blast radius totally blind. Blind people

27

cannot fight in a war; therefore, whoever has the Checkerboard gas will win.

The scientist mentions to a reporter that they are starting human trials with political prisoners. Then, the bomb goes off. Due to a miscalculation, the gas blast is more potent than anyone predicted. It kills the test subjects, and a freak wind current picks up the gas and sends it around the globe in a matter of days. Also, the gas does not blind anyone. It just makes them colorblind.

Generations pass. Eventually, a scientist thinks he has the cure for monochromia. An evil billionaire wants the cure for himself so that he can be the only person in the world to see color. He sends his bumbling brother and his brother's girlfriend to retrieve the formula, which is probably not the best of ideas considering these two are challenged by things as simple as doors. (This is a funny little satire that adds just the right amount of slapstick, with little nods to old science-fiction films of the '50s. I'm pretty sure that alligator pit scene was lifted from *I Was a Teenage Frankenstein*.)

As is the case in almost all of Legge's films, *Monochromia* pokes fun at society in general and at pharmaceutical companies in particular. Add a few jabs at poetry readings and ridiculous laws and you have a wonderful film that shows how the human race tends to take things for granted. My favorite law in the film is the illegalization of Bubble Wrap™ and the depiction of addicts called poppers. Yeah, they love to pop Bubble Wrap™. They are treated like heroin addicts in the film.

Planet Void. A meteor crashes into a planet much like ours and releases a mold that does one thing: It kills every male worldwide. Now, the entire planet is run by women, and they are doing a fantastic job of it.

Lorna Nogueira stars as a woman who works for a company that helps run the planet. One day, as she returns home after a couple of drinks, she is visited by an alien spacecraft.

28

The alien makes her an offer: If she will help him to produce women for his planet, he will help her bring men back to hers. The only question is: Does the planet *want* men back?

In *Planet Void*, the men haven't been gone as long as people have been colorblind in *Monochromia*. They still have memories of their husbands, fathers, and sons, depending on their age.

Their science has progressed in such a way that they can reproduce without men in a lab. They have even experimented with trying to bring men back; however, the mold is permanent, and any male newborn dies so horribly that they eventually stopped trying. With the alien's technology, they can change all that.

But does anyone, regardless of what planet they are from, give anything away for free? What if the solution to the situation is more horrifying than anyone could even consider?

Planet Void is a unique way of viewing the eternal battle of the sexes, and it has a comedic slant.

Crawlers. Celebrating their twentieth anniversary, Alan and Jamie plan to invite a few family members over for a party. Alan couldn't care less, but Jamie wants the party. Their eccentric neighbor Clive brings over a

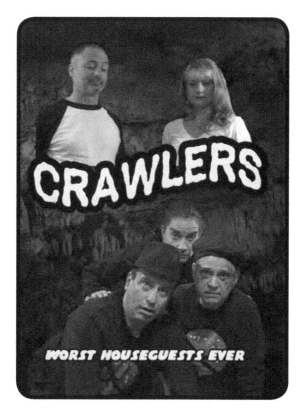

manuscript of snake erotica for Alan to read.

Another typical day.

But at night, odd sounds come from the wall, and then Jamie sees half a man crawling into their room. Alan thinks she is losing it until he and Clive experience the same phenomenon the next day.

Finally, three odd people—Spook, Trixie, and Shorty—appear in Alan and Jamie's hallway. It seems that they are from the future, a far-off time when all mankind lives beneath Earth's surface because humans ruined the planet. They basically are proof of the Hollow Earth theory. (No, I'm not explaining that right now; go read a book or a Wikipedia article. Sheesh!)

Anyway, the visitors escaped

because they were in prison for horrible crimes, such as taking up the whole aisle at the grocery store, wasting food, and, most horrendous of all: putting an empty milk carton back into the refrigerator.

What they don't initially realize is that after generations of living beneath Earth's surface, the sun is awful to them. Even sunglasses don't help. So, they have to find the portal that brought them there in order to go back to the time where they belong.

And then everyone shows up for the anniversary party.

To make everything more fun, in the future, there are animalistic women who are used as hunters. These women manage to find the portal and go after the three escaped convicts.

Crawlers is Legge's final film. He's fine; he's just stopped making movies. Legge is unique in the land of micro-budget filmmaking because he started out using actual film stock.

In addition, he makes comedies. Always fun and satirical, Legge works best when he creates a universe in which his shenanigans can take place. *Crawlers* is a comedy of errors, with a healthy dose of slapstick added to the mix.

I found it interesting that the main characters are given a glimpse into the future, and their first thought is that no one will believe and they will get locked away. They have no plans for using their knowledge to benefit mankind—just an urge to get their unwanted houseguests out as soon as possible. Even when they are questioned by Alan's mother toward the end of the film, Alan tells her that they will probably never bring it up in conversation again.

And she's fine with that.

In the world of micro-budget films, Legge adds a unique voice that is more focused on the comedy, including where to find it and poke fun at it.

A trio from "Crawlers."

JAMES LORINZ:
WHAT'S FUNNY ABOUT IT?

BY MIKE WATT

"Ma, something's happening to me that I just don't understand. I can't think straight anymore. It's like my reasoning is all, uh, twisted and distorted, you know? I seem to be disassociating myself from reality more and more each day. I'm antisocial. I'm becoming dangerously amoral. I've lost the ability to distinguish between right from wrong, good from bad. I'm scared, Ma. I mean, I feel like I'm— I'm plunging headfirst into some kind of black void of sheer and utter madness...or something."
"You want a sandwich?"[1]

Jeffrey Franken (Lorinz) weighs his options.
(Photos courtesy Hotel Broslin. All Rights Reserved.)

One of the great delights is Frank Henenlotter's *Frankenhooker*, the story of a young and heartbroken mad scientist who hopes to reassemble his dismembered fiancée using the body parts of dead prostitutes. The chief reason to watch the movie is the lead performance by James Lorinz. As Jeffrey Franken, Lorinz deadpans the madness around him, muttering to himself as the sole company on his decent. As he sorts through a bin full of legs, he happens upon an arm. "How did that get in there?" he asks, flinging it aside. As wonderful as the movie is, it's difficult to even imagine it with any other actor playing Jeffrey.

Lorinz is also one of the

1 This is, of course, the classic exchange between Jeffrey Franken and his mother, played by Louise Lasser. "It was funny because of her reaction," says Lorinz. "I think they only had her for a day or two. She was a lot of money per day, but they wanted to put a name in. Sandy Dennis was originally supposed to be in that part. Now, I'm saying that monologue to [SF artist Gabe Bartalos]! He put the thing on, the dress, because we had to reshoot. Couldn't reshoot her stuff, so they reshot mine."

highlights of the nasty cult classic *Street Trash*. Directed by Jim Muro and written and produced by Roy Frumkes (*Document of the Dead*), *Street Trash* is a dirty, skid-row-horror satire about life among the wretched refuse. While bums literally melt into toilets, poisoned by Viper wine, Lorinz's Doorman harasses mob boss Nick Duran (Tony Darrow).

> **NICK DURAN:** *"You're a fucking dead man, you fucking rat. You know what a fucking dead man is? That's what you are, a fucking dead man."*
>
> **DOORMAN:** *"Yeah? Well I'll tell you something. I'd rather be dead than wear this fucking monkey suit. I look like Bullwinkle."*

"I think people talk about *Street Trash* a lot in the horror community. But as far as the mainstream places go, [my stuff] had the only scenes where nobody was melting or exploding. The mafia guy, [was played by] Tony Darrow—and you know how things go when you're shooting a movie. There are these long periods of nothing going on. They're setting lights, you're sitting around. We were kidding around. He was insulting me, I was insulting him. We were laughing and having a good time. The director [Jim Muro] was laughing too. He said, 'Why don't you use some of that stuff in the scene?' He picked out a few things that he liked and let us improvise. It must've gone over well because two weeks later, I get a call, and they told me, 'They wrote another scene for you guys.' We somehow became this little bridge, this little subplot to what was going on, which was good! You needed a little humor to break up the 'playing volleyball with a severed penis' and gang rape. It was a good thing to have something in between."

Obviously, *Street Trash* isn't to everyone's tastes. "But we're still talking about it today, thank god. Because *Street Trash* is not everybody's cup of tea. It's hard to swallow. I regret using that term." It's a grimy movie, grimly funny, and unapologetic. But Lorinz's scenes with Darrow are hysterical. The natural banter between the two, even though Lorinz's poor schlep of a worker never really has the upper hand (well, maybe at the end), he never gives the mobster an inch.

"Tony Darrow is a real performer. I went to see his show in Atlantic City, where he'd sing and tell jokes—one of those old-style guys. He told the jokes and was very funny, but a lot of his stuff comes from trying to survive that anxiety. But he's really good at it. He won't let himself doubt. I'm sure everyone suffers from self-doubt, but he doesn't give in to it. He takes over when he thinks he can handle [the job]. We've done a lot of things together. We're friends. We don't hang out so much, but a couple of weeks ago, I texted that I loved him. So, there you go. He gets back to me, [*gravelly voice*], 'Me too, bruddah!' I think we helped each other. He had a much bigger career take-off than I did. But we got noticed. We did *Me and the Mob*, we did *Swirlee* together—the short film I made. We've been trying to do another one! My friend Rocco is a screenwriter, and he's written a few pieces for us to do, but it's hard to raise money unless it's something, you know, exploitive. On the other hand, today you can shoot a movie for $100 if you have the manpower."

As we talk, James's phone rings, and he apologizes for putting me on hold. "Sorry about that; it was Tony Darrow," he tells me. "I told him to go fuck off."

As a budding young filmmaker, Lorinz winding up in the low-budget *Street Trash* as an actor was no fluke. "I went to the School of Visual Arts. Roy Frumkes was one of my teachers. He taught the 8mm Film Production class, my first or second year there. I became friendly with him. And then I couldn't get it. I'm not a technical person. The first year, they teach you a lot of technical stuff—editing, how to touch the film, reading a light meter. I didn't realize that I wasn't really interested in any of that. I was more interested in the creative process, so I wound up leaving. Roy stayed in touch. He knew I was trying to branch out and perform, and he gave me a part in the movie. It was one line. I was sitting outside this restaurant and a mafia guy comes out. I'm supposed to say something like, 'Good evening,

sir'—something stupid just to get me a credit and get going. I didn't really audition for it, he gave it to me."

The outrageousness of the movie gained it notoriety and led many of the principals on strange paths. Muro went on to be in demand as a cinematographer, most notably on shows like *Shameless* and *Southland*. Lorinz, again, hysterical in *Street Trash*, found a role on another grimy production: *Last Exit to Brooklyn* (1989), directed by Uli Edel, with Desmond Nakano adapting the classic tragedy by notorious author Hubert Selby, Jr. (*Requiem for a Dream*). It's a tale filled with sad prostitutes, closeted homosexuals, transvestites, drug addicts, thieves, and (eventually) murderers. It ends with the horrifying gang rape of the principal character, Tralala (Jennifer Jason Leigh, in one of her many impressive roles). Lorinz won the part of a young member of a teen gang working for shady union rep Harry Black (Stephen Lang). Also in the gang were Peter Dobson, Stephen Baldwin, and Sam Rockwell in their earliest roles. Neither Rockwell's character (Al) nor Lorinz's Freddy are

Freddy (Lorinz) and Al (Sam Rockwell) in Last Exit to Brooklyn. *Not a comedy.*

named in the book, but the whole gang is as unseemly as the rest.

Lorinz's big scene occurs midway through, after Alexis Arquette's Georgette, "the Queen," lies bleeding in the street. Dobson recommends putting her in Freddy's car. "Are you serious?" whines Freddy. "I just redid the upholstery."

"Funny you bring that up," Lorinz tells me. "That is *also* not a comedy. At the time, all I had was this instinct to do something that was off or bizarre to make people laugh. Some guys would say, 'Oh, you've got talent!' but I don't know if that's what it was. It was insecurity, anyway.... When I met [Edel], I was wearing an old World War II army coat. I go in, 'Hey, the war's over, let's let bygones be bygones.' When I auditioned for that movie, I wrote my own monologue. There were no sides or scenes, they were just looking for people to play part of this gang. So, I wrote my own monologue—it was pretty funny, and it was real. When I was a kid, my parents were smokers, and they used to throw cigarette butts in the toilet but wouldn't flush it. When I'd get up in the middle of the night to go to the bathroom, [the butts] would be there. I used to play this game where while I'm pissing, my dick was a "Jap Zero" and the butts were Pearl Harbor. So, I'd aim the piss-stream at the filter until it broke open. The tobacco would spill out, and those are the guys—[*screams!*]—as they're dying, you know? So, I wrote this silly monologue about it, and this guy, the director [Uli Edel], I don't even think he spoke English, but he acted like it was the funniest thing he'd ever heard! So, then I got cast in the movie. It had nothing to do with being a tough guy.

I think it was because I connected with him in a way, with the laughter. Whether it's funny or not, you make a German guy laugh...."

Oddly enough, though he did it for the laugh, Lorinz's monologue showed a canny connection not only to the character of a young post-war Brooklyn alley punk, but also to the very subtle humor that would occasionally, beyond expectation, creep into Selby's work. A kid entertaining himself in a depressing situation seems very Selby. "I didn't read the book before I wrote the monologue, though," says Lorinz. "I took a chance and it paid off. But there have been so many times I've done that and the people think I'm nuts. 'Boy, this guy's weird.' And I think I sabotage a lot of things. But I don't know how else to do it! When I try to do it their way or the conventional way, I just come off like everybody else. [Edel] was just crazy enough to recognize what I was doing. That guy—I think he was drunk! I know I was."

Given the sprawling, multi-character narrative of *Last Exit to Brooklyn*, the production split its time between New York and Germany. "Me and Sam Rockwell were like the two extras of the movie. We didn't really have much to do. The other guys went to the big rape scene—I mean, the scene was big. They shot it in Munich, and we stayed here and became friendly. So, one night, me, Sam Rockwell, and Alexis Arquette went out to a diner. We were shooting in Red Hook, took the subway to Manhattan, found a diner, and had breakfast. It was late—five in the morning when we got out. I don't remember anything unusual, but it's interesting to look back on. It was like we were all just getting off a shift from work and grabbing some chow. Look at the lives those two have had since, ya know?"

Lorinz followed *Last Exit* with two films considered iconic for different reasons. In Abel Ferrara's *King of New York* (1990), Lorinz has a small part as cop Tip Connoly, brother-in-law to David Caruso and part of the crew hoping to take down the titular king. After a huge wedding set-piece in which Tip marries his bride (and drunkenly attacks Caruso), he is part of a shootout and chase involving Wesley Snipes and Larry Fishburne, and it ends badly. Ferrara fans love it (I'm also a fan, yet not a Ferrara fanatic), but it should come as no surprise that I prefer the other 1990 Lorinz movie, *Frankenhooker*.[2]

For his part, Lorinz seems genuinely mystified by the accolades he receives for his role. (people with natural timing; go figure). "I still don't understand that one [*Frankenhooker*] because, again, I wasn't trying to be funny," he says. "I was playing it straight. What makes something funny is when you really believe it, right? So, I wasn't trying, but everything I did came off like a gag. Maybe it's my voice? I don't know. I

2   As *Exploitation Nation* has featured bits with Frank Henenlotter and Gabe Bartalos (*Frankenhooker's* special effects foreman), I may have to confess to some bias. Also, I have to confess that about 10 years ago, at Cinema Wasteland, we forced James Lorinz to have dinner with us. We literally dragged him from his table by himself and stuck him in a group of hyper, over-caffeinated strangers. Basically, I bullied him into being my friend. I regret nothing.

think it's instinctual because I didn't learn anything. I don't know how to do stand-up or plan anything out. It has to come from someplace real for me. That's why a lot of that stuff was improvised, because a lot of times, when I tried to do it again, it would fall flat; then you're just doing a joke, you know? I think it also has a lot to do with fear. When you're performing, there's a lot of anxiety. You feel—OK, I'll talk about the elephant in the room. Everybody feels inferior and scared. 'I'm gonna make a fool out of myself!'—that kind of stuff. And that's just me in a grocery store! Imagine being in front of the camera. But if I can make people laugh, I found that it relieved a lot of anxiety. But then it became this unhealthy thing, needing validation. 'Well, if they don't laugh, there must be something wrong with what I'm doing," or 'Why do I have to impress this person?' So, this is a great study in psychology, what we're doing. And fortunately, I've been through enough shock treatments… they're just turning up the voltage now."

Everyone knows that the best way to fight anxiety is to audition in front of indifferent strangers. This is what Lorinz continued to do. As *Frankenhooker's* production continued, Lorinz hit auditions on his off days. One was for a guy named Martin Scorsese. You may have heard of him.

"Scorsese—that fucking guy," James says with a laugh. "I love that fucking guy. Because of him, I wound up in filmmaking! I wanted to be him. I wanted to make his films. I was supposed to have a small part in *Goodfellas* early on. While I was shooting *Frankenhooker*, I got an audition. 'Martin Scorsese wants to meet with you.' *What?* I went to see him, and we talked. You know that Don Knotts movie *The Incredible Mr. Limpet*? He loves that movie, and so do I. So, that's what we talked about.

"So, I read the scene—he has everybody reading the same scene. And it's the scene where, 'Listen, I don't want you selling any drugs!' We do the scene, and Scorsese says to me afterward, 'Listen, I don't know what to tell you; all the parts have already been cast. The part you're reading is going to a friend of mine, Joe Pesci. I guess I could give you one line here or there, but ....' And he was giving me a compliment! I would have taken the one line. Then, he asks me, 'What are you doing the rest of the day?' And I'm thinking, 'Here it comes: the casting couch.' Right?

"He says, 'Our reader didn't show up. Would you mind hanging around and reading with the other people for the rest of the day?' By the 'other people,' he means these big Hollywood names. And I got to see how other fucking people audition! It was eye-opening! Some people are just horrible! Just like me! They didn't even prepare. Some people were really prepared. I remember reading with Vince D'Onofrio, and he came in real intense. All these '80s actors. Jennifer Grey came in. And it was like a gift. 'Listen, everybody's the same. We're all just reading a scene and hoping to get a job.' When I left, I was already feeling good because I had a job. I was working on *Frankenhooker*. But a couple of days later, they call back. 'Uh, yeah, Marty wants to put you in this scene as part of the

Choosing the correct part of the brain to drill away is one of the most important decisions any mad scientist can make. (Photo courtesy Hotel Broslin. All Rights Reserved.)

Lufthansa heist crew.'

"So, first I went to the *Frankenhooker* producers and tell them, 'Look, I just got this part in this big movie.' And they're like, 'Well, it'll help *us* ....' So, they rearranged the shooting schedule; they gave me a week off. It was meant to be one week's worth of shooting. And of course, the *Goodfellas* schedule gets fucked up, they miss the week, and I didn't do the scene. I went to Brooklyn and got fitted and everything! I don't even think I had any lines. I just would have been in a scene with all those guys."

However, things were still brewing. Here's some backstory: In 1988, Valerie Harper and her husband, Tony Cacciotti, sued Lorimar-Telepictures after Harper was fired from her successful NBC sitcom *Valerie* (which, as a further slap, continued without her as *The Hogan Family*). The issue was money, and NBC didn't want

36

to part with any. Enter CBS, eager to start a relationship with TV's *Rhoda*; thus they developed *City,* created by Paul Haggis and executive produced by Cacciotti. *City* was to be a big show and would star Harper as a city manager dealing with crazies on a day-to-day basis.

"When we were finishing up the looping on *Frankenhooker,* I learned I got the part [on *City*]. I was auditioning like everybody else. You go on these auditions for pilots. You never get them. [*laughs*] You do 15 of them and nobody ever gets called back. They hardly ever made it to television, most of them. You do the pilot, they order no episodes, and its done. You get paid for the one show. George Clooney went through a bunch of pilots before he made it big. I mean, it's nice that you're working and getting paid—that you're getting cast—but nobody's seeing any of it.

"So, the guy that cast that show [*City*] was named Paul Haggis—*who's in a lot of trouble!* No, anyway…he saw something in me that he wanted. They flew me out to California to do what they call a 'network test.' They have all the different characters and all the people who are reading for those characters stuffed in the same room. One by one, you go into this room and there are about, I don't know, 20 executives in there. There's a reader in there, and you do your scene. Before you go into the room, you have to sign your contract, which is very frustrating. You think, 'Oh, I'll get this amount of money for this, and that for that, plus moving expenses.' But the thing is, once you're cast, they don't want you renegotiating your contract!

"So, everybody was there, but I was the only one reading for my character. I didn't put two and two together. I didn't know what was going on. There're a lot of politics involved. Somebody wants to use somebody; you don't always get your way. I don't know if this Paul Haggis had a lot of power at the time, because I've been in other situations where I got screwed out of parts. I got the part because Paul Haggis said, 'I want this guy. I don't want you to pick.' It was great. I got a little taste of what it's like to have a real Hollywood job. They went with my character. All I would do is deadpan what they wrote down."

Lorinz was cast as Victor Sloboda, the building's dim security guard. More capable than Barney Fife, Victor never did anything half-assed. To catch the perpetrator stealing office supplies, Victor coats himself in Wite-Out™ to camouflage himself as a wall. "His original name was 'Grady Sutton,' and I remember the director was Howard Storm [who also directed *The Hogan Family,* which was scheduled opposite *City*]—very famous stand-up, did the Borscht Belt, famous director. He was, like, 'What do you think about your character?' And I said I was a little embarrassed by his name. 'Grady sounds like this old guy. I don't know. I was talking about this with my best friend—'

"'Oh, what's your friend's name?'

"'Victor.'

"They didn't want to get involved in using a real person's name, so they used Slobota, which happened to be Storm's grandfather's name when he came over from Europe. So, there's a history behind that character name.

Victor Sloboda—I felt better about that. Not Grady.

"The other thing he said to me—we were talking about what my beliefs were, and he wanted me to play it like a right wing, gun-loving American patriot. I looked at him and said, [*horrified*] 'Oh no! No!' But I said that because I didn't really believe that. And he just said, 'OK,' and he let it go. He was a really good director. Not that I was going to fight him if he insisted on that. But I saw Victor as this kind of dope who had a little bit of empathy. He understands what it's like to be in someone else's position. But he's also ridiculously dumb. Nobody could be that dumb. That's why when I play his lines as deadpan as possible, you believe him and it's funny. I'm not trying to play him dumb. Still, I kept waiting to find out when I was going to get screwed, you know? But everybody was so nice. We would play theater games before rehearsing. It got to the point where, you know, maybe it got too comfortable. So, maybe it was part of my journey to tell me, 'Hey, it's not gonna be that easy.'"

Defying all expectations, *City* only lasted a single season. Though it pulled in record numbers at first, viewership dwindled, and by sweeps week, it was canceled. *The Hogan Family* would last another year. "I don't know what happened," says Lorinz. "They had a huge television star. They figured it was in the bag. Now that I look back on it, though, for the first few months or so we were on the air, we were in the top 10! Oh, this is a hit, you know? Then, it slowly started slipping, and they started changing the time around. This will tell you a lot about the business, because the show kind of got fucked. Many of the shows that were doing much worse all got a second chance. *Seinfeld* wasn't a hit but took off after its second season."

Reminding myself that this is the comedy issue, I ask if he has any funny *City* stories. "One time, my parents flew out to see a taping of the show. It was nice. When you have money, you can do that. I flew them out, picked them up in a limo, put them up in the Sportsmen's Lodge on Ventura Boulevard. No, I'm not going for the luxury, though. We're going for the mid-level. I'm humble. It's good enough for them.

"They have a warm-up before the show. Now, this was an episode where I was going undercover as a woman. There was sexual harassment going on in the city offices. *Sounds familiar!* So, I'm there and I'm all dolled up. I looked pretty good, I have to say. Now, the guy who was doing the warm-up found out somehow that my parents were in the audience. The guy talks to my father: 'Oh, your son plays so-and-so. What do you think? How does he look tonight?'

"My father goes, 'I think he looks *ravishing.*'

"The audience broke up."

That concludes James Lorinz's L.A. adventure. I knew that around that point, he returned to New York. I asked when he made that decision. "When I ran out of money," he says. "I made quite a bit of money on the show, but it got canceled, so I moved back to New York. In hindsight, I should have stayed in Los Angeles; I probably could have gotten another job. But the *City* money ran out and two years later, I'm working as a fucking messenger at a Rockefeller

Center law firm there. I was able to get away with not working for about two years. I had a cheap apartment. But remember, I went to film school and I wanted to be a filmmaker. I wanted to be a writer. I had this money, and I had this idea of Mr. Softee, the ice-cream truck mascot. I said, 'I'm going to shoot this short film, and I'm going to shoot it myself. I'm not going to try to raise money—I have the money. I'm just going to shoot it as cheaply as I can. Back then, what you would do is shoot a scene or two and show it to investors or a studio. I mean, when your main character is a human ice cream cone, it's hard to pitch that. Don't ever use your own money, that's all I've gotta say. That's why I had to get the real job."

The short film he's referring to is *Swirlee*, a marvelously surreal crime film about a man with an ice-cream cone for a head. Lorinz's *King of New York* costar David Caruso is in it. At one point, Swirlee, depressed that no one will take him seriously, decides to kill himself by taking a hot bath. There is literally nothing like this movie.

While the short itself is legendary, Lorinz always hoped to turn it into a full-length feature. "Well, you know, I almost got it made a couple of times. Hey, the *Frankenhooker* people liked it, but that fell apart. The one thing they don't teach you in film school, and they should, is how to have a meeting with someone. How do you explain what you want to do to someone who can help you do it? Yes, you want to be an artist, but you still have to make sense to someone to where they say, 'Oh, why yes, I'll produce that. I'll pay you.' I learned it eventually."

Swirlee, for the fascinated, is available to view on YouTube. "I showed it at a film festival not too long ago. Seeing it in a room of 50 to 60 people, I got that idea again, that feeling that it's supposed to be fun, you know? It's fun to watch people see your stuff and laugh with it. Most of them were laughing. It's funny, but it's also serious, which is why I couldn't get the money from Shapiro-Glickenhaus. They kept saying, 'Get rid of the suicide scene.' He wanted to make a children's movie, I found out. Like a G-rated thing. I went through several rewrites and everything. But I just want to shoot the original thing. Rocco wrote the script, and I really like it. It just needs to be updated a little bit. But yes, it's still something I really want to do. See, it sounds easy to make a movie. Get a camera for cheap! But there're logistics involved, there are people you have to get together. It's a little too big in scope. But no, I haven't given up yet. *No!*"

Post-*City* came small parts, including *NYPD Blue* with Caruso and *Mr. Wonderful* with Matt Dillon. But things slowed down further. "I think I booked one job in that time, and it was the first time anyone had a job and just gave it to me without making me audition. 'Here's a job. Want it?' And it's *Robocop 3*. It was great. And it takes away the anxiety of having to audition. This guy, Fred Dekker, he's a great guy. I think he was just a hired gun for this film. It was like Scorsese directing *Boxcar Bertha*. This was Fred's *Boxcar Bertha*. You think actors are making all this money. That was a day rate. And the point is, you're supposed to book at least one of those a month.

"Then came *The Jerky Boys*. That put the final nail in the coffin. *I'm just kidding!"*

For those over the age of 30, the Jerky Boys comprised a pair of comedians, Johnny Brennan and Kamal Ahmed, who would make prank phone calls, often at random, and see how long they could engage the recipient in bizarre, confrontational, or inexplicable conversations. The original Jerky Boys tapes were bootlegged and distributed throughout college campuses. (*Film Threat* was a big supporter, as well as being a big fan of the Red Tapes, which often elicited violent reactions from the owner of the Tube Bar in Jersey City.) "Now that's funny," Lorinz says of Kamal and Johnny. "That's not planned. They didn't know who they were gonna get on the other end of the phone. They rolled with it. Those guys were hysterical. Now, try to script that and it doesn't work."

Lorinz had a New York agent who called him one day, saying they were, somehow, making a movie based on the Jerky Boys. "I said, 'What's the character?' He said, 'It's described as a loser from Queens.' I said, 'Oh, yeah, send it my way.' You know who was also up for it and I beat him out?"

"Tell me," I say.

"Nicholas Turturro. Meanwhile, he gets *NYPD Blue* and gets a career! Joke's on him!"

Still, *The Jerky Boys* can boast that Alan Arkin is in it. "Alan Arkin is the best. Just the greatest. And boy is he sorry he made that movie! *Kidding!* After that, he had a

whole resurgence—all these Oscar-winning movies, one after another, after *The Jerky Boys*. He was such a great guy. Everybody's fawning over him. The guy's a legend, what are ya gonna do? We're talking about *The In-Laws* and all this other stuff. I remember there's this scene where he threatens me. He's the mob boss and I work for him. He threatens me, and I'm supposed to grab his jacket and beg, 'Please don't kill me, Mr. Lazarro!' So, we do the take, the guys call out, 'Reset!' Alan comes over to me, and he says, 'Hey, listen, do me a favor.'

"I said, 'Sure, Alan, anything.' He goes, 'Be careful when you grab this lapel, because this jacket is leaving with me.' He had all these $500 sports jackets, and he was taking all his clothes with him! Who could blame him, right? That gave *me* the idea. I have all these suits in the movie. These

Lorinz as Brett Weir in The Jerky Boys: The Movie.

ridiculous, obnoxious suits. However, they were all tailor-made for me! And I looked great in them. Yeah, they were all checks and obnoxious patterns, but they would have been fun to have. Right? So, I made a deal. You know what? I'm gonna tell you the truth, boy. This is like what the government is doing to us. So, when you're an actor, right, and you're in the union, and you wrap from a production, they say, 'You're wrapped. You're done. Good job. Go away.' I said, 'OK, that's it? We're done?' Done.

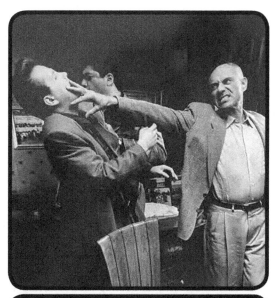

Attacked by Alan Arkin (pictured here with a suit he got to keep) while blocking Vincent Pastore (suit info not available)!
(Copyright © Buena Vista Pictures. All Rights Reserved.)

"Two weeks later, my agent calls me: 'There's one more scene they wanna s h o o t with you.' Great. Well, when you're in the Union, that's called a 'drop pick-up,' which means, those two weeks they let me go? I have to get paid for. Back then, it was a good chunk. He says, 'They wanna know if you'll do them a favor.' Well, they don't want to pay me for the two weeks. He says, 'What do you want?' You know, in exchange for doing this one little bit. I said, 'Well, I want my wardrobe.' *Like Alan Arkin got!* And I wanted the producer, who was the cheapo, to take me out to a fine French restaurant. So, they agreed to do it. I do the scene, whatever. It's a little stupid thing. The guy says to me, 'OK, you can have your wardrobe, but you can't get it until the show locks.' OK, I understand. I get it.

"So, he takes me to this French restaurant that's right near the set. They're still shooting on 86th Street in Manhattan. I went over to see Kamal and my friend, Peter Appell. We're having dinner, and it was the night of the Bronco chase—O.J. running with the Bronco. All of a sudden, everybody's left the table. That wasn't what I had in mind. But I wanted to watch the chase too. So, we ate at the bar. Nobody's eating—everybody's in the bar watching TV. Because he's running from the cops! It was that night. So, flash-forward. It's a month later. The movie's wrapped. I have to call. 'The movie's wrapped. When do I get my suits?'

"The producer says, 'Well, I've got some bad news for you. Somebody forgot to tag the clothes, and everything went to Goodwill!'

"And, God, that's just the perfect ending! So, no clothes—I don't even remember what I ordered. I think I had a hamburger. So, that's Hollywood for

41

you. I don't care to call them out now, because they're not going to hire me again."

There's another stop on the James Lorinz journey here, playing down-on-his-luck Jimmy Corona in the 1994 film *Who Do I Gotta Kill?* (a.k.a. *Me and the Mob*). "*Me and the Mob* was another great example of the spirit of independent filmmaking. I made a good friend; his name is Frank Rainone. He was a filmmaker trying to make a film called *Brooklyn State of Mind*. He saw me, I guess, in *Frankenhooker* or whatever, and he wanted me to play his guy. We became friends, we were hanging out. It was taking so long to get his movie funded, so he said, 'Let's raise a few bucks and shoot a short film.' Just to do something. So, we did this thing called *Writer's Block* on 16mm, and it was fun. And this guy really knew how to produce, by which I mean that he knew how to get people together and make them get things done. After the screening, two guys came up and said, 'What are you doing now?' Two guys—two proctologists—got the whole things started. After my exam, they said, 'We'll give you $25,000 to make this movie.' [*laughs*]

"That's literally how it became what it did. They said, 'We want to get into the movie business.' From there, we rented an office and started writing the script. We each wrote a version. Rocco wrote a version. Originally, it was called *Who Do I Gotta Kill?* They changed the title on us. They didn't think that title was commercial enough. They were trying to pair it with *Married to the Mob*. Some smart guy in the promotional department came up with that dazzling title. I think *Who Do I Gotta Kill?* would have been a little more interesting...."

Jimmy Corona is a hapless writer who joins the mob "to make ends meet." The film teams Lorinz up again with Tony Darrow for some hilarious dialogue. It costars Vincent Pastore (*The Sopranos* and literally every other mob movie ever made) and features cameos by Anthony Michael Hall, Roy Frumkes, and Steve Buscemi. And staring as Jimmy's girlfriend, Lori, who breaks up with him during mid-boisterous coitus because he's too exhausted to give her a reason to stay, is one Sandy M. O'Bromowitz (a.k.a. Sandra Bullock).

"What happened was, at the time, Sandra Bullock and I had the same manager. He had us and Anthony Michael Hall. Tom Chestaro was his name. He was responsible for me getting an agent, which is what managers are supposed to do. So, when we were making the movie, he suggested using Sandy. She wasn't a big star yet. I happen to think it's one of the ballsiest thing she's ever done. That 5-minute sex scene where she's talking the whole time—that was one take. A lot of actresses would have said, 'Fuck that. I'm not doing that.' And then, of course, she took off. She did *Demolition Man* right after that, I think."

But control is key, and if you aren't holding the purse strings, you don't always have the control you need. "As you probably know, people get ripped off when they make a deal with some shady distribution company. For example, Steve Buscemi is in it. I was friendly with him. He said, 'I wanna work with you. I like your work, but I don't want to be credited.'

The role that won Sandy Bullock her Oscar! From Who Do I Gotta Kill?

We put that in the contract, did the scene. He was great. He's funny. I don't care. But you'll also see *his face* on the box art, which is completely illegal. He could sue them, I guess, if he wanted to. But we're not talking about a lot of money. I don't care what they use on the box, I just wish they'd put out a decent copy of it. A lot of copies I've seen look like they were shot off the fucking screen of a movie theater. What's funny is, the guy that shot the movie, Adam Kimmel, was an up-and-coming cinematographer [on *The Ref* and later *Jesus' Son*], and the movie looked good when it came out in the theater. It would be nice if other people could see it like it was meant to."

After a series of small parts and TV appearances, Lorinz needed a break. "I took 12 years off from acting, OK? To raise my daughter, I worked in the car business. I did nothing. Now I'm trying to start again. Only four or five years in."

If you want to know what James has been in *lately*, well, let's just say Marty didn't forget about him. "The woman who cast *The Irishman*, Ellen Lewis, remembered me. She goes, 'I just wanna let you know, Marty totally remembers who you are, and we're bringing you in, but there really isn't much left to this movie.' So, they brought me in; I think I read one line, but the same thing: I wrote my own monologue, and I didn't tell her. I just turned to the cameras in the audition and went into it. And I knew it went well because she interrupted my story and said, 'Wait, are you serious?' And I was on and they could believe what I was doing. I think he saw that. You know?"

The Irishman would consume a couple of years of Marty's life, telling the story of Jimmy Hoffa and his friendship with a hitman (Pacino and De Niro, finally sharing screen time in

43

something worthwhile). It was highly anticipated. Everyone in New York is in it. So, Lorinz was excited to be involved. Still…he was *supposed* to be in on the Lufthansa job.

"But then I never heard from anyone. I'm thinking, 'Shit, I fucked it up,' because they're shooting the movie, and then the movie was almost over! Months later, I get a call. 'Yeah, listen, they want you to be part of Jimmy Hoffa's meeting. They want real actors because Al's gonna improvise and these extras don't know what they're doing.' You know, they want a different caliber of…. Sure enough, I go there, and I was very grateful. I didn't give a shit because I was there. I was in the audience of Hoffa's speech. There was a scene where I got to shake Pacino's hand. It was the only line I had in the movie and I think it got cut out. [*laughs*] I figured, if only it would have stayed in, that would have been my moment. I worked on this line for so long, and it had to do with my monologue. Pacino's coming through the crowd, and I grab his hand and go, 'Hey, Jimmy, I just got a new Buick!' He stops and goes '*Whooooaaaa!*' So, we did it four times, and he did the same thing. I never got any direction. One guy they told to calm down. 'Hey, listen—' He's doing this whole monologue. They're like, 'No, no, just say hello.'

"But then I get a call a week later, and they bring me back with two other guys, and now it's four years later [in the story]. So, I go from being this guy who looks like Sach from the Bowery Boys in this crowd, to a guy

The Cast of City. Top (L-R) Tyra Ferrell, Todd Sussman, Stephen Lee, LuAnne Ponce. Bottom (L-R) Lorenz, Mary Jo Keenen, Valerie Harper, Liz Torres, Sam Lloyd. Copyright © Paul Haggis Productions/MTM Enterprises. All Rights Reserved.

44

in a suit who runs his own chapter of the union; one of Hoffa's fucking mob guys. He's yelling at us in the office. I still have it—a bead of spit comes off Pacino's mouth and lands on my lapel! This man—lemme tell you, my friend, I was a big De Niro man my whole life, but now, Pacino, what I saw him do in that scene—this guy is 78 years old! And he is screaming and fucking going off, right? And they call 'Cut!' and the guys had to help him up into the chair. He gave his all to this fucking thing.

"But that's not the part that got me. They turned the camera around, so it's not on him, it's on us. It's time for our reaction. This is the time the star goes home and you get some guy reading the lines. Right? I've been through it a million times. Pacino stayed there and did the same intense performance for us! Then, I was like, 'Oh my god, this is what being an actor is like.' You forget it's Al Pacino. You see a guy using his skill and doing his job seriously. This guy is so concerned with the film that he wants to make sure the reactions to his performance are him! I was so blown away by it. Now I know why this guy is so great!

"Seeing Scorsese come out and he's laughing! I've never seen a guy have such a good time. And I'm thinking, 'That son of a bitch.' Meaning: *It's fun to make a movie!* That's the whole idea, right? Forget about making $40 million dollars. (Although that helps.) You're making a movie with your friends. You're telling jokes. He came out and he's looking at us. Scorsese's direction to the five of us there, he looks at us and goes, 'Welllll, you've really done it this time, haven't you, boys?' He was having fun!

I was like, man, *this is the job*. I'm going overboard on it. I don't know.

"We're all in tough times. I'm at a crossroads here. But when I was in that room, Pacino in front of me and De Niro behind me, at this point, I was like, 'Oh my god, these guys aren't any different than I am.' I'm not saying worth—we're all doing the same thing here. We're acting. This illusion that you can't be something or can't achieve this—*oh, there's no way*—it's wrong. Especially in film, everything is broken down, scene by scene, moment by moment. You know? It's just a matter of being repetitive and doing it again and again. Getting it down. And you have two of the greatest actors ever and you're witnessing this. I would say, yeah, it was life-affirming."

"We are all struggling." That's the message of 2020, isn't it? We're all in this together, like it or not, and life is always harder than it should be. The virus shut down the world, so with conventions more or less still on hold, it's tougher than ever for Lorinz to meet with his adoring public or even keep up the morale to work. Over the phone, we commiserate about the stay-at-home lifestyle. "This is, like, my third week at home, which I love. I don't mind it at all. I'm one of the few people who loves to stay home all day and do nothing."

Of course, I agree. "I love working out of the house."

"I didn't say anything about *working*, my boy," Lorinz says. "I'm talking about staring into space. Between that and masturbation, the day goes by!"

Work for everybody is slow. Check Facebook and the

announcement of a new production elicits equal parts anticipation and horror. (Did you shoot wearing masks and social distancing? Did the PAs wash their hands before setting out yesterday's leftover lunchmeat?) "The only thing I got left, I did this movie called *The Stay.*" *The Stay* is directed by Kevin Rhoades and Bobby Francavillo, and it's written by Mel Hagopian and Richard Harlost. It's currently listed as "In Production," but hopefully, that will change soon.

"Listen, after you have these fucking tragedies, nothing comes out. Movies just take a bath. But this was a little independent film, shot in New York, and I have a very different kind of role in it. It's not funny at all. I play a guy who runs a hotel. This couple comes by and I'm trying to sacrifice her soul to the devil so I can get the soul of my sister back, whom I lost years ago. I'm doing all sorts of satanic prayers, and I'm wearing a cape! [*laughs*] I don't know if it'll ever see the light of day."

Still, the struggle continues. You can work with every famous person in the world, but that won't necessarily translate to your own success. "I wish I could have more comedy roles offered," Lorinz says. "My manager sends me mainly for, you know, deranged FBI agents, or, uh, let's say, shy rapists. No comedy in there at all. Still, I have to say, every project I've ever worked on, I've come out with one good friend. I can say that about everything I've ever worked on. I'm actually working on a project Kamal is doing. He's made five feature films. This one is called *Crash the System*, and he decided that he's going to do a series. There are a lot of new outlets, and people need content. Apple TV and all this shit. And if you can make something that's halfway decent, you might be able to sell five or six episodes. Fame isn't so important when it comes to TV. People just want to watch something. Gotta have 'content.' I can't even explain what it's about. It's about two government agencies. One is doing experiments with mind control and sound—it's very current now, how to control people and opinions, make people do things they don't want to do. I have no idea what it's about, but I'm fascinated by it. Kamal is the real deal. He gets his own money, makes a movie for $70,000. We shot in my apartment here! My wife and kid are here. I'm still trying different things."

We talk for a little bit longer, about life and other stupid shit. I complement his timing again, recalling another favorite moment from *Frankenhooker*, and again, Lorinz is demure. "Remember, all that mumbling I'm doing was on a small set with a limited number of people. It wasn't like they were laughing at it. I didn't necessarily have that motivation to try harder or think 'This is working, that's not working.' Frank, the director, was just picking and choosing stuff that I was giving him to just cut away to. Being on camera all the time, when you're doing some stupid thing where you're walking across the room and turning on a television set, here comes that self-doubt, that anxiety, you know?"

Go to James's Facebook page and like and follow him. Stop by *The Stay* page and let them know you're interested.

We're all in this together.

GOONS ON THE MARCH
THE FOUNDATION OF BRITISH COMEDY

BY MIKE WATT

If you're anything like me—and really, who isn't (and if you're not, you should be)—you like funny things. At the very least, you like things that are funny. There is a difference, though the modern instrument capable of measuring this difference has yet to be invented. And while we've spent a goodly amount of time discussing American humor and what it is and what it might not be, we've managed so far to thoroughly ignore comedy from other countries. But that's Americans for you.

Many straight lines (and even more crooked ones), and at least one traveling in an ellipsis, can be drawn from the famous BBC radio comedy *The Goon Show*. Produced and broadcast on the national BBC Home Service from 1951 until 1960, *The Goon Show* was, primarily, audio anarchy courtesy of three men: Harry Secombe, Peter Sellers, and Spike Milligan. With non-sequitur plots that meandered through scenes and gags, the Goons made nonsense into an art.

> **HENRY CRUN (Sellers):** *"Here, hold my elephant gun."*
>
> **MINNIE (Milligan):** *"I don't know why you brought it. You can't shoot elephants in England."*
>
> **CRUN:** *"What? Why not?"*
>
> **MINNIE:** *"They're out of season."*

While Sellers did quite well in the U.S. and became a worldwide star, the others didn't achieve the fame of their fellow performer. Secombe was the funniest of the three in terms of physical grace—not a great strength on the radio but beautiful to watch in *Penny Points to Paradise* (1951), the Goons' film debut, in which Secombe mimes a heart surgery performed by a novice surgeon.

Milligan is another beast entirely. He's difficult to sum up, both as a person and a performer. Milligan's personality tended toward chaotic, which informed his comedy. The Goons' penchant for ending a sketch by colliding with another sketch in lieu of delivering a punchline was a huge influence on, for example, *Monty Python's Flying Circus*.

THE
BED SITTING ROOM
Directed by Richard Lester
(Starring in order of height)
Rita Tushingham Dudley Moore Harry Secombe Arthur Lowe Roy Kinnear Spike Milligan
Ronald Fraser Jimmy Edwards Michael Hordern Peter Cook and Ralph Richardson

These live shows drove Lester to seek a career in film, in which you are afforded a second take.

After the success of these shows, Lester and the Goons decided to screw around and made the short experimental comedy film *The Running Jumping and Standing Still Film* (1959). More of a tone poem made without rhymes but not without meter, *The Running Jumping and Standing Still Film* was plotless and featured folks popping in and out of frame, doing silly things, and generally being the Goons. In turn, the film was nominated for an Academy Award, which it did not win.

What the film did, however, was delight the notoriously difficult-to-delight John Lennon, then of The Beatles and, logically, still alive. Lennon and his mates—McCartney, Harrison, Starr, Sacco, and Vanzetti—loved *The Running Jumping and Standing Still Film* so much that they personally invited Lester to direct their first two films, *A Hard Day's Night* (1964) and *Help!* (1965). In between, Lester directed *The Knack…and How to Get It* (1965), and that, as well, is certainly a movie.

But, notoriously, *Help!* was so admired by Hollywood upstarts Bob Rafelson and Bert Schneider that they chose to rip off its entire *raison d'être* with *The Monkees* TV show. As The Monkees were intended to be a "Prefab Four" or

Indeed, *The Goon Show* was an important base for most of the great British comedians of the '70s and '80s. All of the Pythons, whether they were at Cambridge (Cleese, Chapman, Idle), at Oxford (Palin, Terry Jones), or Terry Gilliam—all of the Pythons doted on the Goons and adopted the chaos, taking the anarchy to their bosoms, both individually and in a group setting.

In 1956, Sellers caught a variety show directed by an American named Richard Lester and enjoyed it enough to enlist Lester, listless on a list that included Liszt, to hopefully translate the Goons for television. They came up with *The Idiot Weekly, Price 2d* (1956), which folks liked, and they followed it up with two more things enjoyed by people who like that sort of thing: *A Show Called Fred* (1956, very funny) and *Son of Fred* (1956, harder to find).

a Beatles-by-committee, the free-spirited *Help!* was a perfect template. Fortunately for all, the band The Monkees quickly outgrew the oddly formulaic structure and went on to be important voices in American rock 'n' roll. More importantly, the band and the show were successful enough to allow Rafelson to partially fund *Easy Rider* with Jack Nicholson and Dennis Hopper, thus paving the way for New Hollywood. So…were it not for the Goons, we might not have gotten *Taxi Driver*. Such is the wonder of history.

Yet the tangled skein further tangles! Lester and Lennon would make *How I Won the War* (1967) with future Phantom of the Opera Michael Crawford, which, though it was intended to be the ultimate anti-war movie, is virtually unknown today. Also virtually unknown today, though sadder, is the unofficial Goons movie, *The Bed Sitting Room* (1969), possibly one of the funniest movies ever made and ever likely to be made. So, you might as well give it up now.

All seriousness aside, *The Bed Sitting Room* is an astonishingly funny post-apocalyptic comedy. It was based on a play written by Milligan and John Antrobus and adapted for the screen by John Wood.

In the film, Great Britain plugs along against a red sky and green landscape littered with villages of burned-out cars, mountains of shoes (none of which match), hills of broken crockery, structures made only of doors beside upright doors lacking surrounding structures. We encounter the BBC (Frank Thornton[1]), a man

wearing a tuxedo from the elbows up and singed long johns below. He crouches behind a hollowed-out television and begins his broadcast. "Today marks the third or fourth anniversary of the misunderstanding that led to the Third World War, which lasted 2 minutes and 28 seconds up to and including the signing of the peace treaty, fully blotted." The war has left over 40 million dead in Europe alone, and the mere 20 people left alive in Britain are advised by a pair of policemen (Peter Cook and Dudley Moore)—flying along in a balloon-powered Volkswagen—to "keep moving" so as to avoid being targets of an unlikely follow-up strike.

Lord Fortnum of Alamein (Ralph Richardson) confesses to his doctor, Bules Martin (Michael Hordern, who holds a "Defeat of England" medal for failing to save the regency from the bomb— "I tried to catch it, Your Majesty, but one of your corgis bit me"), that he feels he may mutate into a bed sitting room.

> **MARTIN:** "Atomic mutation. A lot of it going about."
>
> **FORTNUM:** "What should I take for it?"
>
> **MARTIN:** "Three guineas for the rent."
>
> **FORTNUM:** "I was hoping you'd give me a prescription of breakfast for a remedy against malnutrition."

There are lots of mutations, as well as marvelously absurd performances by Secombe, Marty Feldman (in his film debut as Nurse Arthur), *Willy Wonka*'s Roy Kinnear, Rita Tushingham, and the always marvelous Arthur Lowe. It's a movie

---

1   Also known as Frank Thornton Ball, best-known as Captain Peacock on *Are You Being Served?*

with credits listing the cast members in order of height.

"Nobody ever got the point about what it was about," Milligan told Bernard Braden on ITV's *All Our Yesterdays* in 1988. "What we were trying to say through all this laughter and fun was that if they dropped the bomb on a major civilization, the moment the cloud had dispersed and sufficient people had died, the survivors would set up all over again

2   Washbourne also played Mrs. Pearce in *My Fair Lady* (1964).

and have Barclays Bank, Barclay cards, garages, hates, cinemas and all…just go right back to square one. I think man has no option but to continue his own stupidity." Ultimately, *The Bed Sitting Room* is a testament to the stubborn and inherent stiff-upper-lipness of the British Empire.

But while the Goons and *The Bed Sitting Room* failed to find the coveted attention of Americans, their offspring received plenty of love. Cook and Moore were part of a stage show called *Beyond the Fringe*, which never clicked for me but clicked with the embryonic Pythons. (Cook never caught on in America, but his unctuous half-a-costar Moore had an inexplicable success following the hit film *Arthur*, after which he was never as good again. Harlan Ellison used to tell a funny story about an inebriated Moore hitting on a mobster's

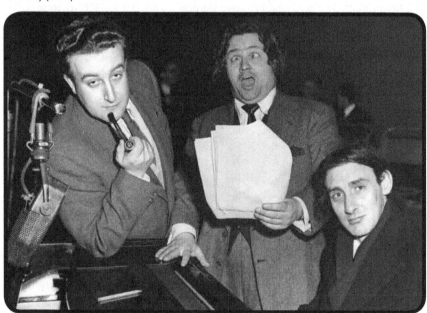

The Goons: Peter Sellers, Harry Secombe (middle), Spike Milligan.
(Photographer unknown. Which is all the better for him to hide. He knows what he did. All rights reserved.)

girlfriend. Ellison was funnier than Moore.)

The future six-person troupe banged on with such shows as *Do Not Adjust Your Set*[3] and *At Last the 1948 Show*, refining sketches and ideas. Their paths crossed again with Feldman, who had his own show (with credits by Gilliam) and wrote two seminal Python sketches, "The Bookshop" (in which he seeks the book *Ethel the Aardvark Goes Quantity Surveying*) and "Four Yorkshiremen" (cowritten by Cleese, Chapman, and Tim Brooke-Taylor).

> **YORKSHIREMAN 1:** *"There were 160 of us living in a small shoebox in the middle of the road."*
>
> **YORKSHIREMAN 3:** *"You were lucky. We lived for three months in a brown paper bag in a septic tank. We used to have to get up at six o'clock in the morning, clean the bag, eat a crust of stale bread, go to work down at the mill 14 hours a day week in-week out. When we got home, our Dad would thrash us to sleep with his belt!"*
>
> **YORKSHIREMAN 4:** *"Luxury. We used to have to get out of the lake at three o'clock in the morning, clean the lake, eat a handful of hot gravel, go to work at the mill every day for tuppence a month, come home, and Dad would beat us around the head and neck with a broken bottle, if we were lucky!"*

---

3   This show gave us the Bonzo Dog Doo-Dah Band, featuring Neil Innes, also known as the Seventh Python, the first Rutle, the ninth Beatle, and the eleventh Earl of Lint-upon-Tweed. Innes links Monty Python's *Holy Grail* to The Beatles' *Magical Mystery Tour*, and both link to Eric Idle's The Rutles.

Feldman also wrote a sketch in which a man struggles with a screaming, fussing creature inside a giant wicker crate. "It's a thing," he explains, covered with bloody scratches like a proud mama puma. To identify it, he turned to *Olsen's Standard Book of British Birds* with no luck, followed by the Audubon *Book of Wildlife*. He didn't find it. "Then, I looked in the Book of Revelations," he says, with a tip of his hat. "Found him."

Feldman's funniest solo film is *Every Home Should Have One* (1970), a satire of the Mary Whitehouse "indecency brigade" that led to the creation of the "video nasty" censorship hysteria of the mid-1970s. In the film, Feldman is an ad man in charge of creating a "sexy new image" for Mrs. McLaughlin's Frozen Porridge. Whitehouse is ridiculed mercilessly in one sequence in which a parish council watches entire programs simply to count the offensive moments.

All of the Goons are dead now, as is Dudley Moore, Peter Cook, Marty Feldman, Graham Chapman, Terry Jones, Moe Greene, and all of the heads of the Five Families. And as Brother Theodore would say, "I don't feel so well myself."

While the Goons were not a household name in America, don't mistake their lack of merchandising for an absent impact. Were it not for *The Goon Show*, there would have been no Firesign Theatre. Lacking the Firesign Theatre, what would *The National Lampoon Radio Hour* have sounded like? Certainly, *The Muppet Show* would have been less zany. The Goons gave nonsense the permission it needed.

BERGMAN'S BRAINCHILD

BY BILL WATT

I have a litmus test—well, actually, several tests—that I use to determine whether you and I should have an ongoing relationship. It sounds slightly off-putting, I know, but let me explain before you dismiss it. Let's start with movies: If you tell me you hate *Citizen Kane*, I understand. *Kane* is a difficult and, in some ways, obscure story; even polarizing, to be honest. It's not for everyone. However, if you tell me you hate *Singin' in the Rain*, or if you think there is a better Robin Hood than Errol Flynn, I'm sorry, but we can never be friends. We can discuss why I like *Citizen Kane* and why you do not, and we can eventually come to terms with agreeing to disagree, but no amount of dialogue will suffice to persuade you of my feelings for *Singin' in the Rain* and Errol Flynn, and I will equally never understand your dislike.

In a similar vein, I think the Marx Brothers are the funniest group, and Groucho the funniest single performer, of all. I also loathe the Three Stooges. I think you see where this is going. Like *Citizen Kane*, the Marx Brothers are an acquired taste, but if you like the Stooges, have a

nice life and don't bother me. I have strong feelings about art, music, and literature as well; I don't think it's necessary to go into all of that here. If you're confused in any way by the forgoing, get comfortable, because confusion is what this little piece is all about.

All of that being stated, I'm going to attempt to talk about a "comedy group" for which I have a fondness, even though I am not devoted to them, nor am I particularly well-versed in their total output. I haven't listened to their albums in years and have never seen them in concert. I know next to nothing about them as people, and I suspect I would not understand a scintilla of their opinions on virtually any subject. I'm not even going to mention them by name until the end of the article, and maybe not even then, as an homage to their work. I will distribute a few clues as we proceed. Some are direct quotes ("I'm looking for the Same Old Place." "Oh! You must mean the old Same place! It's right out back, sonny. Here's the key"). Some are paraphrased because that's how I remember them. I point this out for the sticklers who may read this article. Yes, you, Bobby Stickler—don't think I don't see you.

I love verbal confusion. When someone recently asked me, "Have you lived here all of your life?" I replied, "Not yet." When my wife said she had to make an appointment to see a doctor who was part of a medical practice, the receptionist asked, "Which doctor?" Without blinking, my wife said, "No, a real one." Maybe we've been together too long.

Little cohesion and a great deal of chaos is the stock-in-trade of the group I've not named. With a nod to the Marxes and a tip of the beanie to Spike Milligan and the Goons, the foursome (that's a clue) embarked on a semi-safari of oral and aural vinyl semi-sanity. "Bring your mukluks in out of the cornstarch and thaw them by the cellophane."

Anarchy is a word often used—too often used, if you ask me—to describe comedy that doesn't adhere to the formula of setup, punchline, reaction, and on to the next joke. These guys kicked formula in the ass by throwing everything into a paint mixer and leaving the mixer unlidded. What spewed forth was a carefully, or perhaps carelessly, adroit mélange of malaprop, puns, mangled metaphors ("So, lieutenant, what brings your big flat feet sniffing around here?"), and silly similes, as well as an overlapping (and sometimes underlapping) dialogue of radical thought disguised as inspired gibberish, if that makes no sense. And that's just the tip of the Bergman and the Ossman cometh. They were testing the comedy city limits from here to Austin, and they had a proctor for the test. As a result, defining their brand of alternative comedy is like catching water in a colander: A few drops will adhere, along with a few strands of pasta, and they're hell to scrape out if you let them dry.

Since these bozos were primarily recorded rather than seen, it's to be reckoned that they saw themselves as kin to radio personalities. The genius of radio was its limitation; a true collaboration between unseen narrators and the imagination of the listeners was necessary. You had to fill in the blanks; no one could tell you that the program was too violent, too sappy, too risky, or too... anything. Since radio and its big sister, the phonograph record, were dependent on electricity, the major drawback was power failure. A serious interruption might cause you to wait for the electrician. These clowns were not insane; they knew that they had faces and talents made for radio, or rather, vinyl. The signs were all there: "Antelope Freeway - 3 miles."

For me, myself, personally, in the first person, singularly and alone, I enjoyed their forays into detective parodies—whimsical excursions that edified and confused without enlightening, yet leaving you wanting less, or at least not more. Of particular note was *The Tale of the Giant Rat of Sumatra*, based on an allusion to a case in a Sherlock Holmes story. I'll not bore you with the details of the story, because I've forgotten most of it, but a few drolleries from said *Rat* should pique your interest. When Hemlock Stones is hired by a beautiful young woman named Violet Dudley, he offers to take her purse, coat, dress and kah-nickers (The K is not silent), after which, he exclaims: "Why, without your clothes, you're naked!" When the case takes Stones and Dr. Flotsam to America, they go to a restaurant. The waiter takes their order, and Stones says, "I'll have a Coke. I understand you have it in bottles." The gags are innumerable, if that's your idea of a good time. The story abounds in bounders (look it up), blunders, and puns galore (a minor character whose granddaughter dated James Bond). It is actually an excellent parody of a Holmes story. No, really. "Antelope Freeway - 2 miles."

I also have a soft spot (It's in the hollow of my throat) for *The Further Adventures of Nick Danger, Third Eye*. This was presented, I believe, on the B-side of their second album (*How Can You Be in Two Places at Once When You're Not Anywhere at All* [Columbia, 1969]). I like to think that they had the most fun with the parodies rather than the logical corkscrews of the extended sets usually found on the A-sides. I also like to think that bluebirds and mice are excellent seamstresses; make of that what you will.

Nick Danger is the classic hard-boiled private eye: perpetually broke, invariably put upon by life, and constitutionally clueless. "Now the gum was on the other shoe." A cross between Raymond Chandler's Philip Marlowe and radio's Johnny Dollar, Nick becomes involved in a case because a scuzball named Rocky Rococo[1] (Think Peter Lorre in *The Maltese Falcon*) tells Nick that a woman from Nick's past is in trouble.

1   An example of the troupe's love of inside jokes: Many of their routines were peppered with "deep cuts" from The Beatles, and this was a reference to "Rocky Raccoon."

The following paraphrased dialogue ensues.

> **ROCKY:** *"Perhaps you remember Marian Faber?"*
>
> *[Nick says no.]*
>
> **ROCKY:** *"You might know her as Audrey Farber?"*
>
> *[No again.]*
>
> **ROCKY:** *Betty Jean Bialowski?*
>
> **NICK:** *Oh, you must mean Nancy?*

The entire thing is done in the form of a radio show from the 1940s, complete with commercials. I sprinkled this article with clues that mostly come from this particular episode. Here is one more: "You can sit here in the waiting room, or you can wait here in the sitting room." And another: "You don't have a key!" "No, only have half a key…I had to split it with the sound effects man."

It's impossible to summarize, or even winterize, the soup to nuttiness of their comedy. I confess that I didn't (and still don't) get a lot of it, but then, I never understood my brother's fondness for olives and orange juice either, especially at the same time! These pliers-wielding, non-dwarf crushers shredded norms and wheat with equal gusto, much like their silly walking cousins across the pond. I've been told by Legions (Harry Legions, a mechanic of my acquaintance) that it's better to listen to them when high. Well, I've listened to them on the roof of my house, and despite the distraction of an inquisitive squirrel, that method did not increase my understanding.

In the end, maybe it doesn't matter if we "get it." Comedy, like any other art, is not dependent on getting it. **Fire**, air, earth, water—no matter what **sign** we're born under, we need **theatre**, and absurd is often preferable to mundane or even tuesdane. Art of any kind is created because it must be. The compulsion to write, paint, or compose is inherent to our nature. We need it regardless of whether we acknowledge it. As much as it is possible to "know" anything, know this: "We are such stuff as dreams are made on."

I haven't scratched the surface because that leaves marks, but I hope you'll follow the signs I posted along the way. "Antelope Freeway - 1 mile."

This is dedicated, with fondness, to the memory of Peter Bergman.

Clockwise from top left: Phil Proctor, David Ossman, Peter Bergman, and Phil Austin.

ADDITIONAL THINGS BORN UNDER THE FIRE SIGN

BY MIKE WATT

We're all about additional information here at *Exploitation Nation*, and if your appetite is sufficiently whet, here's some more.

One of the best introductions to Firesign Theatre is *Firesign Theatre: Weirdly Cool* (2001). This is a recording of their live reunion show, featuring classic bits like "Porgie Tirebiter" and "Not Insane."

A personal favorite here at *ExNat* is *J-Men Forever* (1979). *J-Men*

repurposes and redubs old adventure serials to tell how the Caped Madman (Republic Pictures' Captain Marvel) and friends attempt to prevent the Lighting Bug from taking over the world. Firesign members Philip Proctor and Peter Bergman wrote the script, and their voices star.

For an even deeper cut, the whole four-man troupe wrote 1971's *Zachariah*. In this Western-comedy-musical based on Hermann Hesse's *Siddhartha*, John Rubinstein stars as the titular greenhorn who starts an odd, homoerotic relationship with a surprisingly sensitive and young Don Johnson. Country Joe and the Fish are in this film as the Cracker Band, so be warned.

Of course, you could always go and grab the albums, all still available on CD, audio download, and direct delivery to your fillings (or so I'm told).

CAN'T STOP THE SONIC

BY MIKE WATT

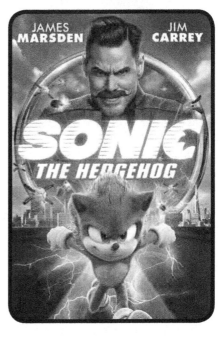

The Indie Mavericks Behind the *Sonic the Hedgehog* Movie and How the Film Is Secretly a Murder Comedy (Don't Tell Anybody!)

Once upon a time, I did publicity for indie film distributors. One of the first ones I ever handled was a great indie comedy from 2003 titled *Hey, Stop Stabbing Me!* It was easily the best thing I handled that early on, and it remains one of my favorite movies. The filmmakers behind *Hey, Stop Stabbing Me!* represent a rare success story that is all too important to today's morale.

In the film, world history major Herman Schumacher (Patrick Casey) is left momentarily homeless when a Good Samaritan picks him up and then drives off with all his belongings. Via an odd stroke of luck, Herman lands a place to live, a potential girlfriend, and a job all in the space of a couple of hours. His disparate roommates all deny the existence of a basement monster that steals socks, his girlfriend is an indiscriminate nymphomaniac, and

his job as a degree-holding world historian consists of digging holes in the middle of a field with other world historians. Having already taken the place of a former roommate who "moved out or joined a cult," Herman suspects that one of the other house-dwellers—probably Blaine—has been murdering people and burying them in a garden. The main clue is a half-dozen signs with painted-on

57

names marking what are possibly graves. But who can worry about that when something is stealing socks?[1]

Directed by Joshua Miller (his professional name for many years was Worm Miller) and written by Miller and Casey, *Hey, Stop Stabbing Me!* was conceived and shot during the pair's junior year of college and represents their future-life anxieties. "We were basically projecting fears of the future," Casey says on the film's commentary. "Herman is unprepared for everything that happens to him, and that's how we felt. Worm was a film major, I was a TV major, and it was a pretty real fear that we weren't going to get jobs after we graduated. Which is why everybody [in the movie] has a double major of something and comparative lit: the least practical fields of study."

And yet, the movie was a good enough résumé piece to take with them to L.A. After a chance meeting with Scott Hillenbrand, who hired them to do the behind-the-scenes extras on the must-be-seen *Piñata: Survival Island* (starring *Buffy*'s Nicholas Brendon, Jaime Pressly, and a giant killer piñata), the pair had a good run with the *National Lampoon's Dorm Daze* film series (including the very *Stabbing Me*-esque *Transylmania*) and a little cult thing Miller created called *Golan the Insatiable*. Recently, the pair took their skills in dark absurdist humor and turned it into *Sonic the Hedgehog*.

So, don't let anyone tell you that indie filmmakers can't make a difference![2]

Not to put too fine a point on it, but the pair may have more in common with the titular hedgehog than his blue fur. They, too, move fast. "We actually wrote *Hey, Stop Stabbing Me!* so quickly that I basically don't even remember doing it," said Casey. "We'd tried to make a different movie that summer, kind of a '90s-style indie talkie comedy, which we shot part of but then had to bail on it when it became apparent we would never finish due to cast availability. And the car that the plot revolved around died! We couldn't finish the movie without the car. The movie was cursed.

"So, we went back to Josh's house feeling frustrated. We somehow started with the title *Hey, Stop Stabbing Me!* and came up with pretty much the whole story in one delirious afternoon. The way we built the script, actually, is that we sort of made a list of all the cool locations we had access to and all the cool filmmaking

---

1   Not to give too much away, but the sock-stealing is perpetrated by a fuzzy something called "Perkutzitwuzzel."

2   Zero sarcasm intended

tricks we'd figured out how to do in the course of the sketches and shorts we'd previously made. And we tried to incorporate them all into one thing, so it was sort of a greatest-hits reel. It's a miracle it came out as coherent as it did. I don't remember how long we spent working on the script, but I wouldn't be surprised if it was less than a week."

"It was coming off a period in college where we were cranking out a quickie, no-budget feature every summer vacation," said Miller. "I don't think it occurred to us that was a crazy thing to be doing every year. But *Stabbing Me* was indeed both a 'greatest hits' and the culmination of many lessons learned the hard way. For one thing, due to that previous film imploding under frustrating scheduling conflicts, I remember that we crafted *Stabbing Me* so that most scenes would only feature Pat and one other actor at a time. And we created characters specifically based around which of our friends were most readily available. Andy Kriss wasn't even in the previous movie we were trying to make but wound up playing the second lead in *Stabbing Me* when we found out he was in town and unemployed all summer. I was originally going to play three different characters, but we cut that down to two when another one of our friends revealed he also had nothing better to do that summer."

The difference between *Hey, Stop Stabbing Me!* and many similar low-budget comedies is that it feels like it has a plan. The movie has a beginning, middle, and end, and it isn't padded with endless improvised babble. "It was definitely very thought-out, though I don't think we would have labeled it as such back then," said Miller. "We were so young that we were still figuring out what kind of story structures and comedy style worked best for us. It felt like we were winging it. But we were building off what worked and didn't work with each film. With *Stabbing Me*, we wanted to put the whole thing together in kind of a 'farce' model, where the movie was composed of numerous running bits and one-note subplots that would get pushed one narrative step forward each time we visited it, all building up to a third act where they come crashing together. We could kind of feel our style gelling into place in a way it hadn't previously."

"In the years since then, the process has changed," said Casey. "Now, for instance, we outline! Back then, if we wrote ourselves into a corner and abandoned a project, it didn't really matter. Now, people are waiting on our scripts, so we have to do things in such a way that we actually finish them (especially when we already took money). People's jobs depend on us!"

Where the pair excel—and this applies to everything they've done— is that they know when to end a joke. Rarely is a gag drawn out beyond the point of being funny. They also favor absurdist humor over the scatological, obscene, or drug-related. In short, they avoid taking the easy way out when going for a laugh and employ a Chuck Jones sense of timing and sight gags based on obliviousness but not stupidity. It's a delightful surprise.

For Miller, *Hey, Stop Stabbing Me!* was a turning point. "I think

Stabbing Me also has the distinction, for us personally, of being the first feature script we fully wrote together as a writing team. We'd cowritten several features prior to *Stabbing Me* (including the previous failed movie), but they were written in more haphazard ways, often with us not even in the same state at the same time (due to college). One of us would write a big chunk and then hand it off to the other. Or one of us would kind of take the lead, and then we'd work together editing it later. I think *because* we had to write *Stabbing Me* so quickly, in order to shoot the damn thing before summer break ended, it was the first time we really sat down and wrote the whole thing together in a room—i.e., my parents' basement."

The experience emboldened the pair. They fled Minneapolis for Los Angeles. Cue the music. "When we first moved to L.A., Josh and I got an apartment together. He worked at a sandwich shop, and I worked at a video store. So, between the two of us, we had all of life's necessities for two young filmmakers. I met Scott Hillenbrand [a producer-director who works as a team with his brother, David] at the video store, where he was renting some movies for research. I schmoozed him and told him that I was a screenwriter, so he asked to see two scripts. I sent Josh over to their office with a printout of two scripts (the one we thought was good *and* the one that would eventually become *Dorm Daze*, which we needed to get to that magic number "two scripts"), and then they called the next day to say they wanted to buy *Dorm Daze* and shoot it as their next movie. Then, they also hired us to make the *Piñata*

special features basically as a way to toss us a little extra money because we were still desperately poor (We did not get paid a lot for *Dorm Daze*)."

National Lampoon Presents Dorm Daze and its sequel are little ensemble comedies set in a college dorm (and on a cruise ship in the second installment). What the first film lacks in raunch, it makes up for in extreme enthusiasm. It's a farce, but because it had the *NatLamp* stamp, folks expecting nudity and *Van Wilder* may have been disappointed. "The highs of working on *Dorm Daze* were twofold: The first was being gainfully employed as screenwriters at such a young age," says Casey. "We were just kids! The second was making a lot of friends on set. We were in the cast of all three movies in minor roles, so we were on set most of the time, hanging out with a cast our age. We had very little creative input, considering that we were writers who were on set all the time, but fun times were had. The low points were watching the completed movies."

Miller picks up the thought. "Comedy is such a specific and subjective thing, which we did not fully appreciate moving out to LA. We thought our script was pretty straightforward, but really, it was not. It was an extremely unusual script for a 'college comedy.' It was very *us* in a way that got lost in translation in the hands of someone else. With the *Dorm Daze* sequels, we at least knew what we were getting into ahead of time. Unsurprisingly, of the four films we made with the Hillenbrands, *Gamebox 1.0*, a kind of Y.A. sci-fi thriller (and not a comedy) is our favorite from that period in our careers. We have a soft spot for that one."

But don't get the idea that either man is ungrateful. "I don't want to make it seem like we were miserable," says Miller. "We were happy to be working on *anything* at that age, with movies getting made and distributed, but we were also extremely eager to move on and start doing our own thing, where we could retain some creative control. They were *extremely* fun to shoot, and we're still good friends with many of the actors from those films."

Still, with age comes perspective. For Casey: "It's taken a while, but I think we've finally made enough other stuff that we can look back on the *Dorm Daze* trilogy fondly as an experience, even though they're not exactly classics."

Again, I personally love *Transylmania*, but mainly because it contains several homages to *Hey, Stop Stabbing Me!* For example, there's the "removal and replacement of an impalement object" bit that will never *not* be funny.

For folks who followed the evolution of the pair from indies to *NatLamp* associates, imagine our surprise when *Golan the Insatiable* premiered on Fox. The massively entertaining animated series involved the titular demon, who hangs with his human acolyte, a goth girl named Dylan. And yet, *Hey, Stop Stabbing Me!* was the catalyst.

"*Golan* was the project that reoriented our career back to where we had wanted to be when we moved to L.A. on the heels of *Stabbing Me*," says Miller. "So, it makes sense that *Stabbing Me* was directly responsible for the show. It started at a real

low point in what barely felt like a 'career' for us. We were making so little money writing scripts that we couldn't cover our embarrassingly meager expenses. So, we had a lot of side gigs. Pat was working for a video game company, while I was cobbling together paychecks writing for various websites when the guys at *Something Awful* tracked me down and said they were big fans of *Stabbing Me*. This conversation led to me writing humor pieces for *Something Awful* once a month. Golan quickly became a recurring character that I used. Our friend Dan Balgoyen, who worked for Depth of Field, kept suggesting that Pat and I turn the character into an animated TV show. But we were such nobodies that it felt like a pie-in-the-sky suggestion. Shockingly, a right-place-at-the-right-time moment occurred when Fox was looking for weird, cheapo animated shows for a late-night programming block, and Dan was able to get the concept in front of them. Even more

going from an upbeat story about a misanthrope and her demon, to a video game movie about a super-fast blue hedgehog, but you go where the wind takes you. Miller and Casey were brought aboard the production back in 2016 and remarkably remained the writing team (with Oren Uziel) throughout the film's history. This may not seem like a big deal to anyone outside the industry, but as William Goldman wrote in *Adventures in the Screen Trade*, one of the undeniable axioms is that "the writer *always* gets fired," often for no other reason than the axiom itself. Yet Miller and Casey remained through multiple drafts and are on board for the sequel.

shockingly, Fox bought the show."

"*Golan* felt like we were finally getting back to being 'us'—the sort of cheerful approach to comedy with fun horror aspects built in," said Casey. "That's what all of the no-budget movies we'd made ourselves were, like *Hey, Stop Stabbing Me!* and *Sledgehammers at Dawn*. We called them murder comedies. We thought we were onto something with the style we'd developed, but we couldn't seem to ever get one made professionally. So, it felt like a miracle when Fox bought *Golan* and we actually got to make it pretty much how we wanted it: dark and destructive, but with a cheerful tone and some sweetness hidden inside. *Golan* was really a godsend, and it finally allowed us to get good representation and get our foot in the door with the studios. We would never have gotten *Sonic* without *Golan*, that's for sure."

It would seem like a strange move,

Strangely, for two guys who still aspire to murder comedies, the pair found themselves under few restrictions. (Maybe they didn't have as many pot or lesbian jokes in the first draft as James Gunn had for *Scooby-Doo*.) "As for 'strict guidelines' for *Sonic*—not really?" said Casey. "This was a project where I think the studio didn't really know what a Sonic the Hedgehog movie should look like. They left it up to us, along with director Jeff Fowler and producer Toby Ascher, to figure it out, and the four of us had a surprising amount of creative freedom. Of course, we also originally wrote it to be more PG-13, but the studio wanted PG to maximize box office, which meant toning down some of the action and language. Most notably, they wouldn't let us have Tom ever fire his gun. He only shot robots! But apparently that was too much. In the finished film, he just smashes robots with wrenches and stuff." A fair complaint, I would imagine. Anyone familiar with the game knows the hedgehog goes around strapped. "But ultimately, making it PG was the right choice because kids really love it, and the action is still a ton of fun, even without any of our trademark geysers of blood, like from *Hey, Stop Stabbing Me!*"

But there's a certain confidence that comes to you when a movie you made exceeds expectations. "All the time we were working on *Sonic*, I would say to Josh, 'I just hope this makes a lot of money so anytime someone doubts our judgement, we can just shout out *Sonic*'s total box office and win the argument.' I haven't actually just blurted out '$300 million!' in a meeting yet, but it's only a matter of time."

That 'creative control' is ellusive. Both Casey and Miller undertstand that. The next things that come out of them will likely not be titled *Sledgehammers at Dawn*, and we are all the poorer for it.

"[It is] probably not a surprise to anyone, but it is much easier to get projects going that are based on something," said Miller. "The vast majority of the gigs we've had post-*Golan* have been adaptations or remakes or attached to some kind of brand. Some of those were a lot of fun, but it is always more rewarding when it is something you're building from scratch. A few years ago, we did a 12-episode Christmas horror-comedy anthology for Blumhouse and YouTube Premium called *12 Deadly Days*. The show was created by our friends Jennifer Raite and Chris Cullari. We had no money to do it, and no one had YouTube Premium back then [when it was called YouTube

Red], but we're super proud with how it turned out. And a few of the episodes wound up with a *Stabbing Me* tone."

Casey continued, "We've got an upcoming movie at Universal titled (at least for now) *Violent Night*, a Christmas-themed action comedy— sort of a return to our classic murder comedy genre, but with much higher production values! It actually was a really, really old idea of ours that we kept thinking about after the experience of doing *12 Deadly Days* (We probably would've done it as an episode if we'd gotten as second season for that show). We'd never pitched it to anyone in all these years because we thought maybe it was too stupid, but as it turns out, it may have been exactly stupid enough! Hopefully, the studio is able to figure out how to shoot it even with the whole COVID thing. We're also working on writing the sequel to the *Sonic* movie, which is very exciting. Can't reveal any details here, though! I guess we can drop one little tidbit: Sonic will go very fast." [SPOILERS!]

Finally, they put me at ease. "And we're currently talking with a distributor about getting *Stabbing Me* rereleased and back out there for people to see. Hopefully, we'll have some news about that soon!"

(And you ingrates will probably go with a different publicist!)

Sonic the Hedgehog, starring Jim Carrey and James Marsden, is currently the second-highest grossing film of 2020. Miller doesn't think it affected them. "Aside from having to hire interns to pretend to be us and answer our interview requests, very little has changed in our lives."

THE (SELF-ADMITTED) FUTILE AND POINTLESS NATIONAL LAMPOON MAGAZINE

BY MIKE WATT

Despite a rough start, *National Lampoon Magazine* was the face of new comedy in the '70s. While it ran from 1970 to 1998 (That late terminus may come as a surprise to many), its hey-day was its first decade, when it influenced comedy writing first and foremost, eventually turning into a laugh-factory empire that produced books, radio shows, live performances, and theatrical films. It brought together such great comedians as John Belushi, Harold Ramis, Bill Murray, Gilda Radner, Michael O'Donoghue, Christopher Guest, John Hughes—the list is figuratively endless. Throughout that first decade, *National Lampoon* was the high-water mark for humor.

In the decades since the magazine's shuttering, the nostalgia for edgy comedy—"You can't tell that joke anymore," rail we on the southern end of aging—produced two feature films telling the magazine's sorted story. *Drunk Stoned Brilliant Dead: The Writers and Artists Who Made National Lampoon Insanely Great*, written by Rick Meyerowitz, was adapted as *Drunk Stoned Brilliant Dead: The Story of the National Lampoon* in 2015 as a straight documentary film directed by Douglas Tirola. *A Futile and Stupid Gesture* (2018, directed by David Wain and written by Michael Colton and John Aboud) is a star-studded biopic based on Josh Karp's book of the same name, which focused more on *National Lampoon* cofounder Doug Kenney. Not surprisingly, given the narratives of both books, the films cover much of the same ground and contain many of the exact same beats.

Both films begin the story at Harvard, where freshman Doug Kenney met sophomore Henry Beard. They wound up editing the famous-in-Harvard magazine *Harvard Lampoon* and were the first to actually bring outside attention to the college mag after *Vanity Fair* hired them to do a parody of their publication. There were no guidelines beyond the edict that the fashions had be given center stage. *Vanity Fair* paid $7,000 for the parody, but the icing was the opportunity to include a subscription card for *Harvard Lampoon*. This increased readership exponentially and led to the creation of other parody magazines (including one of *Playboy* that broke publication records). Satisfied by their success, Beard and Kenney (and the undersung Rob Hoffman) were convinced they could take a humor magazine to the national level.

They licensed the "Lampoon" title from Harvard and took their pitch to New York magazine editors. Only Martin Gerald "Matty" Simmons at Twenty First Century Communications took them seriously. After assembling a team of "dangerous" writers, including Chris Miller, Brian McConnachie, British comedian Tony Hendra (a member of the 1962 Cambridge University Footlights Revue alongside John Cleese and Graham Chapman, and who had performed on *The Ed Sullivan Show* several times with his partner, Nick Ullett), Anne Beatts[1], and the volatile Michael O'Donoghue (and later, P.J. O'Rourke, John Hughes (whose work was often the dirtiest), Michael Reiss...), Kenney hired Michael Sullivan and the underground artist collective Cloud Studios. Kenney was taken with Sullivan's crowd because they hung out with artists like R. Crumb and Vaughn Bodē (the latter of which would contribute *Cheech Wizard* cartoons to the mag). Their art direction on *National Lampoon* was to make everything crazy, psychedelic, and ugly. Kenney insisted on including a duck (whose grinning bill was filled with a disturbing amount of human

teeth) as a mascot, thinking it would be on-par with the Playboy Bunny. The look was terrible, undercutting the witty and often intellectual black comedy writing.

After seven issues, Simmons demanded that Kenney fire Cloud Studios, which Kenney grudgingly did, and hire Michael Gross as the new art director. Gross's take was to embrace the mag's satire, arguing that the deadpan parodies were the magazine's strengths, so undercutting the sharpened words with ugly psychedelia was working against them. The bulk of the articles were based on skewed nostalgia for the '40s and '50s—the decades that comprised the childhood of the writers. They wanted to skewer the white, middle-class America that whitewashed its racism and sexism. Gross felt the look should embrace that nostalgia, to the point that

NatLamp writer Ed Bluestone's most enduring legacy. The "Dog in Danger" cover.

1 Beatts, who was introduced to the magazine via her relationship with writer Michel Coquette (They were hooked up by *National Lampoon* editor Sean Kelly), has a great line in *Drunk Stoned...*: "I got into comedy the same way Catherine the Great got into politics: on my back."

the naturalistic Norman Rockwell imagery made you look twice to find the gag. With the look established, the writers focused on the comedy. (This naturalism is what attracted *Café Flesh*'s Stephen Sayadian to the mag; Chris Miller recommended him to the similarly screwy *Hustler*.[2])

Roundtable editorial meetings were held at local bars, where the goal was to make editors Beard and Kenney laugh. Drug and alcohol use was encouraged. Looting the nostalgia of the '40s and '50s resulted in classic black comedy pieces like "The Vietnamese Baby Book" (by O'Donoghue, featuring infant benchmarks like "Baby's First Wound" and "Baby's First Funeral"), Hendra's "Wife Tasting" piece, etc. Writers were given real freedom and rarely edited. (Take, for example, anything written by '80s patron-saint-of-cringe John Hughes, although his "Child Pornography" bit—sex images ostensibly drawn by children as stick figure couplings—is at least funny in concept.)

Kenney also ran with the Italian-style *fumetti* (comics), calling them "Foto Funnies" and using the actual staff writers in photographic comics and word balloons, often placing them in absurd situations with nude female models brought in from the outside. The nudity became the magazine's biggest selling point, something that was lost on none of the staff.

The mix of high-brow and low-brow sometimes worked against the magazine. There were no boundaries. The writers punched down as often as they punched up, mocking minorities, women, and those in poverty, as well as politicians, celebrities, trends, and "straights." Because most of the writers and artists were college-educated intellectuals, the overall tone of the magazine was often smug and self-satisfied. If you didn't get a joke, you weren't part of the club—that went for the readers and the folks who encountered the staff in real life. As Marshall McLuhan says in *Drunk Stoned…*, National Lampoon was "designed to flatter well-to-do nobodies."

As the magazine grew, so did additional opportunities. Hendra and O'Donoghue produced an album called *National Lampoon's Radio Dinner.* The album included "Magical Misery Tour (Bootleg Record)," setting to music John Lennon's famous 1970 *Rolling Stone* interview in which he revealed his "capitalistic excesses" and disappointing Beatles fans worldwide. The success of this album

2   As reported in *Exploitation Nation* #3

led to the plan of a second, which evolved into the off-Broadway live show *Lemmings*, starring Second City performers John Belushi and Chevy Chase. *Lemmings*, in turn, grew into the *National Lampoon Radio Hour*, which was directed by O'Donoghue and marked the beginning of the end of the '70s *National Lampoon* lineup.

Eventually, the success began to weigh on everyone, but Kenney was hit the hardest. A middle-class kid from Chagrin Falls, Ohio, and the son of a tennis instructor, Kenney was hyperaware that he would never really fit in with the "elite" of our society. *A Futile and Stupid Gesture* indicates that Kenney's desire to create the magazine was a last-ditch attempt to avoid joining his father in the country club lifestyle (as, of course, servants to a group that would not allow them to be members). In '73, Kenney vanished from the magazine, leaving behind a note in the apartment that he shared with Beard. The note was simple, more or less saying, "I need to get away." Kenney retreated to Martha's Vineyard ostensibly to write the comic novel *Teenage Communists from Outer Space*. In reality, he was dropping acid and avoiding reality.

Beard resented having the entirety of the work dropped on him. When Kenney eventually returned, sheepishly, to the office, he was not welcomed with open arms by the people who believed he'd selfishly abandoned them. And they weren't wrong. Beard took Kenney's novel, read it, and then chucked it out the building's window. As a consolation for the alienation Kenney was experiencing, Matty Simmons assigned the *National Lampoon 1964 High School Yearbook Parody*, which Kenney would create with P.J. O'Rourke, resulting in one of the highest-selling issues of the mag's history.

After a contractual buyout in which Simmons was forced to buy out Hoffman, Kenney, and Beard (at 21 times earnings, resulting in a payout of $7.5 million), Beard packed up and left the magazine entirely, announcing to the staff, "I hated every minute of this. Fuck you and good luck." Those at the beginning felt that they were stockholders and that Kenney, Beard, and Hoffman were stiffing them out of earnings. Discontent spread through the ranks. Kenney eventually resigned to write *Animal House* with Miller and Ramis. O'Donoghue and Beatts quit over a dispute (Matty Simmons gave Beatts's desk away to writer Michael Simmons in a move no one quite understands to this day), taking the *Radio Hour's* cast—Belushi, Chase, and Radner— and many of the writers over to Lorne Michaels's new late-night comedy show, *NBC Saturday Night* (eventually renamed *Saturday Night Live*). Matty Simmons, who felt the National Lampoon brand was already spread too thin, had just turned down NBC's invitation to develop a TV series. O'Donoghue jumped at the chance, effectively emptying the *National Lampoon* offices with his departure.

With Kenney and Beard gone with the rest of the principles, the magazine underwent another radical change under O'Rourke's editorship. The publication managed to limp along until 1998, continuing to dilute its brand until going under.

The *National Lampoon* logo would be slapped on numerous movies and books over the years[3], with diminishing returns. Kenney would continue to produce films, even after what he considered to be the nadir of his career, *Caddyshack*, a hit-piece designed as revenge against his father but "ruined" by the inclusion of a gopher puppet.

In 1980, depressed and in the throes of severe drug addiction, Kenney was circling the drain. Chase took him on a vacation to Kauai but eventually left him there in order to return to Hollywood for *Modern Problems*. In Chase's absence, Kenney either: (a) fell off a cliff, (b) jumped off a cliff, or (c) was murdered in a drug deal in which the dealers threw him off a cliff. In any event, his body was located at the bottom of the 35-foot cliff called Hanapepe Valley Lookout.

This is basically where both films end.

If you want a straightforward documentary about *National Lampoon*'s history, you could do no better than *Drunk Stoned Brilliant Dead*. Many of the more outrageous stories are animated between talking-head interviews with the principles and fans, including Kevin Bacon, Billy Bob Thornton, and Ivan Reitman. You also get snippets of the *Lemmings* show, a few *Radio Hour* bits, and a lot of archival photos.

Drunk Stoned... is best when you follow it up with *A Futile and Stupid Gesture*. As a biopic of Kenney (perfectly encapsulated by Will Forte), *Futile* follows the same structure as

3   This includes the *Dorm Daze* movies penned by Josh Miller and Patrick Casey, as you've surely already read by now.

Drunk Stoned... is rife with head-scratching decisions, none more so than casting Martin Mull as an "Old Doug Kenney," who serves as the film's narrator. Since Kenney was only 33 when he died, having an aged, wiser Kenney giving us the lowdown doesn't make a lot of sense. This is addressed at the end of the film when Old Kenney meets Dead Kenney. The film also cops to the many, many, *many* inaccuracies and creative licenses taken with the truth. This is presented in a rapid scroll that is well-worth freeze-framing. Among the last of the entries, "Everyone was *much* more racist and sexist than portrayed." Mull's Kenney even admits, "We didn't have many women writing for us, but we didn't have any black people writing either. It's not that we didn't want them. It's just that we didn't think to look."

The casting is as often bizarre as it is dead-on. While Joel McHale looks zero like Chevy Chase, his friendship with the notoriously troubled ~~asshole~~ actor during his time on *Community* helped him absolutely nail his performance. *Star Wars'* Domhnall Gleeson is spot-on as Beard; Matt Lucas makes a suitable Hendra, bringing his bitter complaining to life; and while Matt Walsh looks as much like Matty Simmons as I do, he turns in a good performance as the beleaguered publisher. Thomas Lennon and Natasha Lyonne are so wonderful as O'Donoghue and Beatts, one wishes they'd get their own biopic.

The rest of *Futile*'s cast are largely cameos—Jon Daly is a fun Bill Murray, John Gemberling is a passable Belushi, Seth Green plays three-quarters of Christopher Guest and does so very well, and Erv Dahl does a great Dangerfield but is never given a close-up. So, if you can get past the bizarre central conceit of an "Old Doug Kenney," you'll have a good time with it. (There's no recreation of Kenney's predilection for sticking his dick in unsuspecting women's ears. But, hey, different times, right?)

Regardless of how you feel about *National Lampoon* as a publication, its influence on American comedy cannot be denied. For good or ill, from *National Lampoon* we got *SCTV, Saturday Night Live, Fridays* (to an extent), and a host of movies both favorite and forgotten. If nothing else, it gave us older folks plenty of complaining time—lots of material to boringly lament, "You can't tell that joke anymore."

...Shit, that's a lot of people. Okay: Michael O'Donoghue, Barbara Atti, Brian McConnachie, Len Mogel, Henry Beard, Michael Gross, Matty Simmons, and David Kaestle. Not pictured: Doug Kenney (not yet deceased at the time of this photo.) (Photo copyright © Magnolia Pictures. All rights reserved.)

LEMMINGS: DEAD IN CONCERT
SIDEBAR

BY MIKE WATT

The discovery of *National Lampoon: Lemmings Dead in Concert 1973* arrived with a disappointing payoff. The show was cowritten by several folks, but primarily Sean Kelly, who kept the vague theme together. Ostensibly, the festival was to be the Woodstock for depressives: "Woodshuck: Three Days of Peace, Love, and Death." "We're all here to off ourselves," explains emcee Belushi. If that comes as a surprise to the crowd, the stoned faces betray nothing. Mass death may be a relief.

Though the show was originally performed in halves—part one including the sketches, part two the music fest—what you get on the DVD release is a mix of the two that more or less conforms to the structure on the popular comedy album. It's a wreck.

Highlights include anything Christopher Guest is doing. His James Taylor parody is spot-on. Lowlights are everything else.

The show opened at the Village Gate on January 25, 1973, and ran for 350 performances. This taping came clearly at the end of the run. Belushi in particular looks bored out of his mind. The only time he comes to life is his wonderfully chaotic impression of Joe Cocker doing "Lonely at the Bottom." There's a nightmarish surgery sketch that features a lot of familiar comedy faces, but it goes on too long and it's difficult to hear. Plus, it has Chevy Chase in it, which is a lot of the special's problem.

Now, some of it is admittedly dated. A Joan Baez parody of well-meaning white people "helping" "Negroes" is as cute as the repeated usage of the n-word can be viewed through '70s goggles. The opening song is titled "Lemmings Lament," and if you can decipher any lyrics through the feedback beyond Alice Playten shrieking "We are lemmings! We are CRAY-ZEE!" all power to you, brother.

For a while there, Lorne Michaels was looking to recreate this as a Broadway show. Now, I'm not saying the virus that shut down Broadway was *caused* by that rumor, however....

Anyway, the DVD is available from fine bootleggers everywhere.

THE CRUEL-MEDY OF MR. MIKE

BY MIKE WATT

I am not 100 percent certain that Michael O'Donoghue, master of the terrifying joke, would approve of my title here. While he may find the wordplay forced and unsophisticated, he did adore terrible, labored puns and might have appreciated the appellation for what it is. O'Donoghue, like the insane French playwright Antonin Artaud and his Theatre of Cruelty, was a firm believer that laughter should exact a price, that a cutting remark should draw blood. This is the guy who wrote "Least-Loved Bedtime Tales." His quip has become a motto: "Life isn't for everybody."

Of the *National Lampoon* writers who came and went, O'Donoghue was one of the first and set the standard for black comedy. O'Donoghue's jokes barely reflected light. While he fell into the pattern established by Douglas Kenney and Henry Beard, taking nostalgic looks at the horrors of the white-bread 1950s, O'Donoghue weaponized the format. His

most memorable spread was "The Vietnamese Baby Book,"featuring such landmarks as "Baby's First Wound." He was also fond of sending up Nazis and the Third Reich. As *National Lampoon*'s star continued to shine and the publication found itself sued by bigger and better corporations, one extremely disgruntled party sent

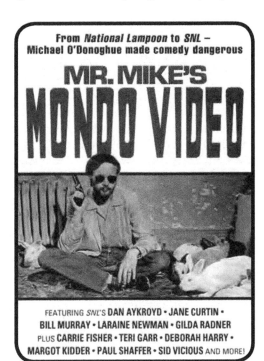

From *National Lampoon* to *SNL* –
Michael O'Donoghue made comedy dangerous

MR. MIKE'S
MONDO VIDEO

FEATURING *SNL*'S DAN AYKROYD • JANE CURTIN • BILL MURRAY • LARAINE NEWMAN • GILDA RADNER PLUS CARRIE FISHER • TERI GARR • DEBORAH HARRY • MARGOT KIDDER • PAUL SHAFFER • SID VICIOUS AND MORE!

71

O'Donoghue a box full of dynamite. Initially, he thought it was a joke. Then, the bomb squad showed up. At first feigning terror, O'Donoghue then seized the box and ran away with it, screaming, "They sent it to me! It's *my* dynamite!"

A sickly kid, O'Donoghue grew up isolated from others. He found the usual solace in books and writing under the dotage of a domineering mother who taught him to, more or less, look down on his bullies, and at school, everyone was a bully to an extent. So, O'Donoghue's intelligence morphed into a dangerous elitism that would often manifest as violent rages over the slightest insult. He was quick to claim betrayal.

At *National Lampoon*, he blew up his relationship with the mag. Tensions had been running high as the various factions of the publication found new success. O'Donoghue was in charge of the *National Lampoon Radio Hour*, which was right up his alley, subverting radio as he had comedy and, previously, experimental theatre. The radio show soon began to outshine the magazine. O'Donoghue felt constricted. He chose a hill to die on: While O'Donoghue and Anne Beatts were on vacation (the two were dating at the time), publisher Matty Simmons loaned out Beatts's desk to another writer. O'Donoghue chose the moment to declare outrage, and the pair walked out.

They then crossed the few blocks to Lorne Michaels's office, where they transformed *The National Lampoon Radio Hour* into *Saturday Night Live*. Michaels had previously approached Simmons in the hopes of adapting the *Radio Hour* for TV, and Simmons had turned him down flat. So, O'Donoghue brought the writing team, which was also its cast, to NBC. These folks included John Belushi, Chevy Chase, Gilda Radner, and a host of others (Christopher Guest, Brian Doyle-Murray, Harold Ramis...). The egress hurt *National Lampoon*, but the publication was already internally devouring itself, so O'Donoghue can't bear the entire blame.

The first episode of *Saturday Night Live* remains legendary. O'Donoghue plays a speech therapist teaching common English phrases to an immigrant (Belushi), such phrases as, "I would like to feed your fingertips to the wolverines." Midway through, O'Donoghue clutches his chest, has a heart attack, and keels over. Belushi, the good student, does the same. Enter Chevy Chase with "Live from New York...!" You know the rest.

O'Donoghue's most famous bit was one he'd done most of his life: impressions of various celebrities having their eyes pierced with red-hot needles. This impression, he mused, was the great equalizer: with red-hot needles in your eyes, everyone sounds exactly the same.

"I don't write for felt," was O'Donoghue's dismissal of the Muppets on *SNL*. Instead, he wrote for revenge. His "Mr. Mike" was a laid-back, smooth-talking, erudite... serial killer. At least you suspected that one lurked beneath the bald head, dark glasses, goatee, and easy speak of a college professor who is about to announce he's poisoned your drink. "Mr. Mike's Least-Loved Bedtime Tales" included "The Little Engine That Died" and the "Tale of the Soiled Kimono" (a drink with a sordid history, topped with a paper crane). All of O'Donoghue's writing had you laughing at the surface and cringing at the slime boiling beneath. "I dare you to laugh," he once said, "and I dare you not to."

O'Donoghue's biggest claim to fame—although, if pressed, I'd say it was the popular *The Incredible Thrilling Adventures of the Rock* (the picture book, illustrated by Phil Wende, in which a rock withstands the seasons in stony silence, page after page) or possibly the Frank Springer-drawn *Adventures of Phoebe Zeit-Geist*, who endures the horrors of her "Perils of Pauline" existence (even during the parts where she's...dead[1])— would have to be *Mr. Mike's Mondo Video*, in which he capitalized on the "mondo" craze begun by *Mondo Cane*. Mondo movies (*mondo* being Italian for "world of") were ostensibly documentaries about "shocking" cultural experiences. Many, if not most, were staged. By 1979, there were about a bazillion of these things.

Mr. Mike's Mondo Video includes a series of sketches featuring famous faces interspersed with one-line gags and stop-motion-animated dream sequences. Highlights include "Crowd Scene: Take One," by Andy Aaron and Ernie Fosselius, in which a director can be heard giving very specific instructions to the background players ("OK, send in another bird").

---

1 In Ernest Pintoff's 1971 hybrid movie *Dynamite Chicken*, O'Donoghue reads segments of *Phoebe* accompanied by a nude model approximating Phoebe's poses. He also contributes a sketch about Sister Filomena, the stripper nun. Paul Krassner is in this too, FYI, along with Richard Pryor and bits of John and Yoko's Bed-In. It's a weird flick.

There's a clip from *The Great Rock 'n' Roll Swindle* of Sid Vicious *not* singing "My Way." On the original video release, the clip is run truncated and silently, because the gag is Paul Anka's people refused to give permission, so the clip is silent. The crawl explains the silence. The reality becomes the joke. "It wasn't a question of money," the crawl explains. "They wouldn't even discuss it!"

The opening bit of throwing cats into swimming pools to prove cats can't drown goes on for too long. However, it's almost immediately followed by Radner, Jane Curtain, Debbie Harry, Carrie Fisher, and Joan Hackett (on the phone) discussing how a man's most disgusting habits turn them on ("I love a man who smells his fingers," says Harry). Plus, you get to see Dan Aykroyd demonstrate that his toes are, indeed, webbed. On the whole, it's a fascinating party disc and exploration into what O'Donoghue found funny.

Coming up next: "Gig Young's Groceries" and "Nazi Oven Mitts."

The special was originally produced to run on NBC during one of *SNL*'s summer breaks. Predictably, the network found it too vulgar and disjointed. Programming head Paul Glazer worked a deal to release the thing uncensored in theaters. It did not do well. However, *Mr. Mike's Mondo Video* was rediscovered through the home video market, which kept it alive and made it into a cult classic.

One of the last bits O'Donoghue wrote was with Mitch Glazer—the movie *Scrooged*. O'Donoghue hated the final film, insisting they'd written a better one. He also cowrote the Dolly Parton song "Single Women,"

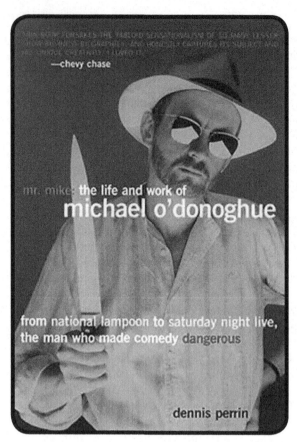

THIS BOOK FORSAKES THE FAUX SENSATIONALISM OF ITS SUBJECT... [illegible] RENDERS [illegible] IN GRAPHICS, AND HONESTLY CAPTURES ITS SUBJECT AND [illegible] [illegible]
—chevy chase

mr. mike: the life and work of
michael o'donoghue

from national lampoon to saturday night live,
the man who made comedy dangerous

dennis perrin

though, it didn't matter because, well... you know.

When O'Donoghue's name is mentioned, someone invariably says, "No one writes comedy like him anymore," but that's demonstrably not true. O'Donoghue's influence can be seen in such pitch-black works as *Rick and Morty* and *Your Pretty Face Is Going to Hell*. Hell, were it not for O'Donoghue, would we have *South Park*, *Family Guy*, or *Bojack Horseman*? (It seems like the edgiest stuff is animated, come to think of it.)

When O'Donoghue joined *SNL*, he spray-painted his office wall with the word "DANGER." That, he said, is what TV comedy lacked, what comedy lacked in general. Lenny Bruce was willing to go to jail for his comedy. O'Donoghue was willing to be blown up. Blowing up is always funny, especially when it happens to someone else.

If you want to know more about O'Donoghue, pick up *Mr. Mike: The Life and Work of Michael O'Donoghue*, by Dennis Perrin. The cover quote is by Chase, whom O'Donoghue went to his grave hating (but, again, dead, so make of that what you will). Though Perrin's book strives to be a typical biography, it's very much like defusing a bomb. Such is the risk of talking about Michael O'Donoghue.

which may have been more surprising to many. When O'Donoghue suffered a massive brain hemorrhage in 1994, many were saddened, but few were surprised.

Bill Murray gave a hasty eulogy for O'Donoghue on the *SNL* episode that coincided with O'Donoghue's wake, and the show reran "The Soiled Kimono" sketch, which seemed to confound the '90s audience. When it was complete, Murray held the drink in his hand. "We all used to be a little afraid of Michael when he was here. But we're not afraid of him anymore. Because he's dead." This, O'Donoghue would have either loved or hated—it was hard to tell with him. Ultimately,

"WHERE'S POPPA?"

BY JUSTIN WINGELFELD

These words are repeated over and over again in Carl Reiner's 1970 film of the same name, as Mama (Ruth Gordon) asks her son Gordon (George Segal) the question dozens of times per day. Either she doesn't understand that Poppa has been dead for years, or she's in denial about it. Regardless, her senility and domineering personality have scared off every affordable caregiver in Manhattan and worn Gordon down, as his personal, romantic, and professional existence is consumed by his oath to his dying father to never put Mama in a nursing home.

But Gordon's promise can only stand so much strain, and now Mama has got to go, one way or another.

One of the blackest black comedies ever made (as well as an early exercise in bad-taste cinema), *Where's Poppa?* might have been a more controversial film by now had it not sunk into obscurity shortly after its disappointing theatrical release. The film was forgotten so quickly that United Artists rereleased it in 1975 under the title *Going Ape*, a reference to the film's repeated jokes involving a gorilla costume. By that time, the film had developed a cult following,

George Segal (left) and Ruth Gordon in Where's Poppa? (Copyright © United Artists, All Rights Reserved)

and the title change only added to its off-kilter mystique.

Considering the film's taboo subject matter and general premise, few approaches would have worked for *Where's Poppa?* other than satirical black comedy. The story could have perhaps been turned into a tragic melodrama, taking a serious look at the psychological toll of putting one's life on hold to care for a parent in mental decline. Or maybe a more lighthearted film could have been made, with a long-suffering son coming to a tearful realization that despite everything, he really does love his Mama. In the hands of Roman Polanski, the story could have possibly worked as a darkly funny horror film.

That the story wound up in the hands of the late, great Carl Reiner makes it all the more surprising. An award-winning television actor and writer, Reiner was better known for his work with Sid Caesar and Mel Brooks, as well as for creating *The Dick Van Dyke Show*. While Reiner's humor often had an offbeat sense of irreverence (Think the bizarre *Dick Van Dyke Show* episode "It May Look Like a Walnut"), it never sank to the dark depths on display in *Where's Poppa?*

It's unclear exactly why he took the job of bringing *Where's Poppa?* to the screen in the first place. Reiner rarely discussed the film outside of expressing his amusement at the fact that he had an official cult classic on his résumé, explaining that for a film to be a cult classic, it has to bomb at the box office upon its initial release and then subsequently find a small but devoted following. While not all films that have achieved cult status were box office bombs, by Reiner's interpretation of the phenomenon, his film sits proudly alongside *Freaks*, *The Rocky Horror Picture Show*, and *Big Trouble in Little China*. I'm not going to nitpick it.

It was the third film Reiner had directed and the first for which he did not also have a writing credit. His directorial debut was *Enter Laughing* (1967),

a semiautobiographical comedy based on Reiner's own novel (and subsequent stage adaptation by Joseph Stein) about a young working-class man who dreams of becoming an actor. He followed that with *The Comic* (1969), a darker-toned comedy about the rise and fall of a pathologically narcissistic silent film actor and his struggles to remain relevant as the movie business changes. *The Comic* starred Reiner's friend Dick Van Dyke as an amalgam of Stan Laurel and Buster Keaton. Both films were box office disappointments and quickly sank into obscurity (Neither has ever been released on DVD or Blu-ray).

What separates *Where's Poppa?* from these previous efforts is the lack of any personal connection for Reiner to the subject matter. The screenplay was by Robert Klane (based on his novel), whereas Reiner had at least cowritten the screenplays for his earlier films. If Reiner were just a hired hand and simply took the job as a way of furthering his directorial career, he picked an odd project to do so. However, it's likely he felt the twisted, mean-spirited humor was right up his alley, and he savored the chance to let loose his inhibitions and really allow the world to see his dark side.

George Segal was reluctant to take the part of hapless son Gordon. Upon reading the screenplay (the same one that likely made Reiner howl with laughter), Segal felt intense trepidation. The subject matter was just too taboo. It may have worked on paper in novel form, but there was simply no way it could be translated to the screen. Whatever Segal's reservations, once he heard that Reiner was on board as director, he

took the part.

Ruth Gordon, on the other hand, would plow into any role with little to no trepidation. Having enjoyed a decades-long career not only in acting, but also writing for the stage and screen, she was a fearless workhorse and had just received an Oscar for her offbeat performance in *Rosemary's Baby*. It seemed no character or story was too outrageous for her sensibilities.

And what a story.

Gordon Hocheiser's life is falling apart due to his promise to his dying father to never put his mother in a nursing home. Things have finally gotten so bad that Gordon has taken to attempting to scare Mama to death by donning a gorilla suit and attacking her in her bedroom. When this doesn't work (Mama simply chuckles at Gordon's funny "joke" after putting an end to the performance by punching him in the balls), Gordon consigns himself to another day caring for Mama (including her usual breakfast of an orange cut into *six* sections, a bowl of Lucky Charms, and Pepsi), which is followed by interviews with potential caregivers and whatever case is on Gordon's schedule in court that day.

Gordon's public defender practice is suffering from his exhaustion. His only clients are a young anarchist (played by a young, pre-"Meathead" Rob Reiner) accused of having severed the big toe of a sociopathic, racist Army general (Bernard Hughes), and a little league baseball coach (Vincent Gardenia) who has kidnapped kids from the ghetto to fill out his team's roster.

After court, multiple potential

caregivers bail on the job (Mama's reputation for being a nightmare is legendary throughout the tristate), but the final interviewee proves promising in more ways than one. Louise (Trish Van Devere), a beautiful, shy young nurse, enters Gordon's office with questionable references and a knack for having patients die in her care. That she and Gordon immediately find each other attractive only sweetens the deal.

When Louise first visits the Hocheiser abode, she is determined to ingratiate herself to Mama. Things don't go well, and Louise flees the apartment, which sets in motion the next major subplot of the film: Gordon's brother Sydney, who lives on the opposite side of Central Park, must race to the apartment to stop Gordon from going through with his threat of finally killing Mama.

Waiting in the park, however, are a group of young men with whom Sydney repeatedly winds up in cat-and-mouse chases on his way to stop Mama from being thrown out the window. The whole situation is a pressure cooker waiting to explode for all the characters except Mama, who just might be a tad more cognizant of her power over her sons than it at first appears.

The plot sounds like the sort of screwball New York comedy that one might expect from Blake Edwards or Neil Simon and Gene Saks. While Breakfast at Tiffany's and Barefoot in the Park had elements of black humor sprinkled throughout, their stories were ultimately about love overcoming the perils of life in Manhattan. Where's Poppa? is way too nihilistic for that kind of gooey schmaltz. No, these characters and the things they do to each other are shocking, and Reiner and Klane are not interested in giving us even a moment of relief from this claustrophobic nightmare with a shoeless spree through the park or an embrace with a rescued kitty-cat. In their twisted world, the park would be littered with broken glass and the cat would have rabies.

In addition to its dark subject matter, the film has a gritty, seedy aesthetic that brings to mind the New Hollywood work of filmmakers like Dennis Hopper and Bob Rafelson rather than a filmmaker who cut his teeth in family-friendly television. Cramped shot composition, offbeat editing, and cluttered set design give the entire film a tense, claustrophobic atmosphere. For a Manhattan apartment, the Hocheiser residence is pretty damn big but somehow feels tiny. Characters seem to barely have enough room to move when interacting. Everyone is in a constant state of trying to breathe and keep calm as the walls threaten to close in on them.

Comedies (even of the dark sort) rarely boast such a level of stress-inducing tension as Where's Poppa? Martin Scorsese's After Hours is the only other film that comes immediately to mind. In After Hours, Griffin Dunne's ill-fated and disastrous journey to Lower Manhattan is as unnerving as a late-night game of Silent Hill, and Where's Poppa? is no less intense. That both films take place in New York City before its economic comeback in the 1990s is more a of a time capsule than most would like to recall.

From the late 1960s well into the

1980s, New York City was a metropolis on the verge of collapsing under its own weight. Crime, infrastructure, and the economy were at the worst levels the city had ever seen. In *The Taking of Pelham One Two Three* (1974), the city cannot afford the $1 million ransom demanded in exchange for the lives of a subway car full of hostages. *Taxi Driver* (1976), *Andy Warhol's Bad* (1977), and *The Driller Killer* (1979) all present characters who have been driven to madness by the pressures of living in Manhattan.

Most of the characters in *Where's Poppa?* have gotten used to their world crumbling around them and are too beaten down to give a crap anymore. Gordon either doesn't notice or doesn't care that the water flows erratically from the showerhead, and having to jiggle the dresser drawer to get it open every morning barely seems to consciously register anymore. The insanity of donning a gorilla suit to induce a heart attack in Mama might just be the closest thing Gordon has had to fun in years.

So, when light comes into his life in the form of Louise and the prospect of happiness is actually at his fingertips, does getting rid of Mama suddenly become more than just a pipe dream? Something has got to give.

Of course, Gordon and Louise can't just have a standard cinematic meet-cute. After hallucinating Gordon as a knight in shining armor (Reiner resists the cliché of adding romantic music, making the moment feel almost creepy), Louise feels so at ease in Gordon's presence that she opens up to him about the ruination of her brief marriage due to the shock of witnessing her new husband's habit of post-coital defecation (or, as she puts it, "He made a caca in the bed"). Rather than being bemused by this story, Gordon instead is enraged at the insult it represents toward Louise ("That son of a bitch took a dump in the bed!"). It is quite easily one of the

Segal (no longer in gorilla wear) and Gordon (right). (Copyright © United Artists. All Rights Reserved.)

suffering brother Sydney.

It's implied that Sydney receiving a phone call from Gordon is a regular occurrence and Sydney's wife is fed up with it, refusing to let him go. He first has to strangle their son to get her out of the way and then later informs her of Gordon's threat to send Mama to live with them. The second method is much more effective.

Despite his wife's warnings, Sydney repeatedly races on foot through Central Park to stop Gordon from following through with his threats to throw Mama out the window. It is unclear whether there is conscious racial or social commentary being made in Sydney's interactions with the group of Black men he encounters in the park or whether it's just Reiner and company pushing the envelope of bad taste again.

A nighttime walk through Central Park in the '70s was fraught with danger (It's still risky to this day), so why Sydney keeps on putting himself through it is mind-boggling. Is he too panicked to think straight, or is it some kind of self-destructive habit he can't break (much like living in 1970s New York City)? These men have gotten used to being stuck at the bottom of a racist and elitist social

screen's most bizarre and out-of-left-field exchanges of dialogue.

Introducing Louise to Mama, of course, is a disaster, and for the first time we get the feeling that Mama might not be as far gone mentally as she would like Gordon to believe. Her obvious dismay at having a rival for Gordon's attention compels her to deliberately ruin the dinner that Gordon and Louise have prepared together. Despite Louise's desperate attempt to win Mama over, Mama proves too intimidating, and Louise flees, enraging Gordon and setting into motion the subplot of long-

ladder and have embraced their place in Manhattan's underworld. Sydney is just passing through.

Even the gang questions Sydney's illogical choice to come through the park, especially without at least a few dollars in his pocket to offer when they inevitably stop him. The situation feels more like a nerdy kid getting taunted by a gang of schoolyard bullies, and Sydney's reaction to them is more of an "Aw, come on, guys" chuckle than an actual fear for his safety. They allow him to continue through the park in exchange for an item of clothing every few hundred feet, resulting in him arriving at Gordon and Mama's building naked.

When Sydney darts nude onto an elevator already occupied by a mousey middle-aged woman, she begins to whimper in fear, and the shot lingers for an uncomfortably long time. A more conventional "edgy" comedy would have the woman either appear receptive or oblivious to this situation (e.g., *Borat's* nude elevator moment), but here, the joke is Sydney having become so desensitized to these ridiculous predicaments that he doesn't even notice the trauma he is causing this poor woman.

After a little guilt-inducing walk down memory lane, Gordon agrees, for now anyway, to spare Mama's life, and Sydney heads back to his wife dressed in Gordon's ineffective gorilla suit, which leads to another racially charged zinger when Sydney has no trouble stealing a cab from little old Black lady despite his attire.

Louise returns bearing Chinese food in the hopes they can have a second try at a pleasant dinner.

Mama is busy watching a fight on TV and has little interest in humoring Louise's peace offering. In the film's most infamous moment, Mama again ruins dinner, this time by yanking down Gordon's slacks and biting his bare ass. An aghast Louise once again rushes off, and Gordon once again calls Sydney.

This leads to the one scene in *Where's Poppa?* that has probably aged the worst. Sydney races through the park (still dressed in the gorilla costume) and as usual, runs into the gang. Only this time, they aren't interested in his money or clothes. Now is the time of the night when they apparently pick a female victim to rape, and since Sydney happens to be here, they might as well include him in the fun for being such a good sport. When a woman does indeed show up and the gang grabs her and holds her down so that Sydney can have his way with her, it barely takes any coercion for him to do so with great enthusiasm. However, the guys immediately run off, leaving Sydney and the woman alone.

Rape is a touchy subject to tackle in the hands of even the deftest filmmaker. It was rarely taken seriously in post-war American cinema. Grindhouse horror films like *The Last House on the Left* and *I Drink Your Blood* were among the few instances when it was treated with some regard for its true level of depravity.

In his play (and subsequent film adaptation) *Play It Again, Sam*, Woody Allen tried to explore the flawed-at-best concept of rape being the secret desire of every woman. While rape/domination fantasy is a potentially interesting subject for a story (even a satirical one), throwing it out there like it is the equivalent of a spanking fetish is problematic and short-sighted.

Rape just isn't funny. The creators of *South Park* tried to create satire by recreating famous rape scenes to express their dismay at Steven Spielberg and George Lucas threatening to meddle with the special effects of *Raiders of the Lost Ark*. Indiana Jones being raped on a pinball machine as a metaphor for the tainting of Trey Parker and Matt Stone's childhood memories may work in conversation, but on screen, it's just grotesque.

The reigning king of "edgy, tasteless humor that takes no responsibility for itself" Seth MacFarlane attempted to one-up *The Simpsons* writers for calling out his derivativeness (a photo of *Family Guy* protagonist Peter with the word "plagiarist" printed underneath it) by creating a fake *Simpsons* ad banner during an episode of *Family Guy* in which Marge narrowly escapes being raped by resident pervert Quagmire. This is not to mention the fact that multiple nude scenes MacFarlane referenced during his disastrous Academy Awards musical number "We Saw Your Boobs" were rape scenes.

Even the late, great George Carlin experienced a rare crash-and-burn moment when he tried to make the case that "anything can be funny" by describing Porky Pig raping Elmer Fudd. The discomfort in the audience during those few moments was palpable.

Rape is a horrific societal phenomenon, which makes it appropriate subject matter for a horror film or drama. But comedy is a different animal. Among the few times a joke involving rape has landed is in the Dudley Moore comedy *Arthur* (1981), when, in response to a prostitute informing him that her mother died when she was six and her father raped her when she was 12, he says, "So you had six relatively good years!" It's a laugh out loud moment, but only because Arthur's inconsideration and refusal to take anything seriously is so shocking.

Like much of the humor in *Where's Poppa?* the joke *is* the depths to which the film sinks. The dark humor of the scene only works depending on how one interprets it. The rape itself is not the joke, it is Sydney's willingness to go through with it that is outrageous. The instant karma occurs when it turns out that the "woman" is actually a male cop in drag, wandering through the park as bait to any potential rapists or muggers. Suddenly, the motivation of the gang egging him on is ambiguous: Did they know their "victim" was actually a cop, and the whole thing just their idea of a prank?

Sydney having to call Gordon from jail (still in the gorilla suit) and tell him he's been arrested for rape is as ludicrous a situation as one could imagine—that is, until the cop sends flowers to Sydney's cell, thanking him for a wonderful time and informing him that no charges will be filed. Turning a rape scene into an absurd comedy of errors takes directorial skill that borders on genius. Whether or not it works depends more on the willingness of the viewer to go along with this sick joke and less on the skill of the filmmakers.

Regardless, if the strain of Mama's care wasn't enough to do it, Gordon's revulsion at Sydney's act is the final straw, and the two part ways, possibly for good. That, plus Louise's decision to leave New York, finally cements Gordon's decision to get Mama the hell out of the apartment, and he informs Louie of his decision in one of the film's funniest moments, having to stomp his feet and speak in tongues before he can finally get the words out.

He and Louise load Mama and as much of her belongings as will fit into the family sedan and head off to New Jersey in search of a home that's right for her. Their first stop is a dilapidated rooming house (A cardboard sign identifies it from the road) where the proprietor and lone caretaker (Paul Sorvino, in his film debut) feeds his overcrowded occupants unidentifiable slop while informing Gordon that he probably doesn't have the room, depending on who might have died overnight. Despite Gordon's seeming willingness to just leave Mama here, Louise has enough concern for her welfare to talk Gordon out of it.

Finally, they find a beautiful home. In a brilliant directorial choice, Reiner shoots the entire climactic scene in one long shot. Mama is lured out of the car by the promise of seeing Poppa. Gordon signs what he has to sign and fulfills Mama's incessant query by grabbing a random old man and plopping him down in front of Mama and muttering, "Here's Poppa." Mama's brief skepticism is put to rest when the old man responds to her asking "Poppa?" by exclaiming, "Mama!" Gordon and Louise then race out of the place to begin their new life together with Mama safely out of their lives. The end...that is, if you are not aware of the film's original ending.

Gordon and Louise arrive back at the apartment to a ringing phone. It's Mama, who has figured out that the gentleman with whom Gordon presented her is not, in fact, Poppa. As Gordon argues with her, Louise can see that there is no way this situation will ever change. Mama will always lord over Gordon no matter where she is. After Louise quietly leaves, Gordon heads to the nursing home and breaks down the door to Mama's room. Instead of strangling or bludgeoning her, Gordon instead says, "Poppa's home," and climbs into bed with Mama. Apparently, Gordon's sexual frustration has hit a point where incest is the only viable solution.

As if Where's Poppa? were not sick and twisted enough, this ending would have been the rancid cherry on top of an already bitter cake. And for a change, it's almost certainly a good thing they cut it out. The official ending is plenty dark without pulling the rug out from under Gordon (and the audience) one too many times.

The film tackles so many touchy subjects that it's a chore to keep track of them all. The frustration that comes with caring for an elderly or special needs loved one, the tenuous family ties that threaten to destroy marriages and relationships, the treatment of the elderly in a society that has no place for them, racial tensions, the anti-war movement, the streak of xenophobia inherent in patriotism, the exploitation of minorities, the constant hazards of living in New York (or any other big city), and the imperfections of simply existing in the modern world—all of it is laid bare.

A film like *Where's Poppa?* strips away the glossy veneer we would normally see in a Hollywood film or television show. In this age of Facebook and Instagram making everything look great all the time, it can be easy to delude ourselves into believing our peers are not as miserable as we usually are. Movies and TV present us with happy white people living beyond their means and dealing with what we now refer to as "first-world problems." Did any of the characters on *Friends* ever have any actual problems? At least *Seinfeld* had the guts to call out its own characters for their repugnant behavior.

That is why black comedy will most likely weather the storm of politically correct, "woke" culture. Comedy is the great equalizer. Locking ourselves out of the house or realizing too late that there's no toilet paper puts us all on the same level. As Reiner's pal Mel Brooks once said, "Tragedy is when I cut my finger. Comedy is when you fall into an open sewer and die." Comedy is being able to laugh in the face of social woes to which we can all relate, be it death, disease, or human cruelty. Laughing at them takes away their power and allows us to look at them from a different perspective. Black comedy is therapy.

Writer Robert Klane would stay within the realms of dark comedy for most of his career, writing several episodes of *M*A*S*H*, the features *Unfaithfully Yours* (1984), *National Lampoon's European Vacation* (1985), the surprise hit *Weekend at Bernie's* (1989), and the Tom Selleck/Don Ameche curiosity *Folks!* (1992), the latter being a watered-down, less harsh take on the same concept of *Where's Poppa?*

Reiner enjoyed a huge box office success a few years after *Where's Poppa?* with the satirical (but far less dark) comedy *Oh, God!* (1976), starring George Burns, John Denver, and Teri Garr. He then began a fruitful relationship with Steve Martin, producing such comedy classics as *The Jerk* (1979), *Dead Men Don't Wear Plaid* (1982), *The Man with Two Brains* (1983), and *All of Me* (1984), which afforded him the opportunity to return to the offbeat comedy he so loved. While his subsequent output was mostly made up of unremarkable comedies, such as the John Candy vehicle *Summer Rental* (1985), the teen comedy *Summer School* (1987), and the erotic thriller parody *Fatal Instinct* (1993), the dark, weird sensibility behind *Where's Poppa?* shone through in parts of each. Right up until his death at age 98, Reiner was an outspoken supporter of liberal, progressive politics and had an unwavering faith in young people. While his humor may have had a streak of dark nihilism, his outlook on life was high octane optimism.

A true cult classic and an example of a film that has grown more shocking with age, *Where's Poppa?* is a rough ride, but it shows everyone involved at the top of their game. While the current state of black comedy or dark humor consists mostly of fart jokes, sex jokes, and profanity-spewing kids, Reiner and company went places few would have dared. Whether they pulled it off is subjective. But they sure as hell tried.

GET CRAZY
HEARTBEEPS FROM
ALLAN ARKUSH

BY MIKE WATT
(INTERVIEW BY ANDREW J. RAUSCH)

After decades of TV work, Allan Arkush is still best-known to film addicts as the creator of *Rock 'n' Roll High School*. Though the film is admittedly a landmark, the young and eager Arkush, along with Joe Dante, originally pitched something different to Roger Corman: *Disco High*. For a while, it was called *Heavy Metal Kids* and, later, *Girls' Gym*. The script developed by Richard Whitley, Russ Dvonch, and Joseph McBride finally landed on a musical style, but Corman originally wanted Cheap Trick or Todd Rundgren. It was Paul Bartel (*Eating Raoul*, but later) who suggested The Ramones. The shooting schedule was brutal enough to send Arkush into exhaustion near the end, but a classic was nonetheless created.

For my money, Arkush made two follow-up films that cement his place in film history: *Heartbeeps* (1981) and *Get Crazy* (1983).

Written by John Hill (*Quigley Down Under*), *Heartbeeps* tells the story of two "faulty" service androids who fall in love, escape their repair warehouse, and roam the countryside. Val Com 17485 (Andy Kaufman) is a valet (with a specialty

in lumber concerns), and Aqua Com 89045 (Bernadette Peters) is a hostess companion with a specialty in poolside parties. Their "malfunction" is that they are slowly becoming self-aware. Deciding to ignore their programming to await repair, they set out to see the rest of the world. They construct a little droid, which they name PHIL, to act as a spare-parts wagon for their journey. They are also joined by Catskill, a stand-up comedian bot who never stands

Andy Kaufman as ValCom-17485 and Bernadette Peters as AquaCom-89045 in Heartbeeps.

up and who smokes cigars and spins one-liners out the side of his face.

They are pursued by an insane Crimebuster bot—a rolling tank that whistles patriotic tunes while blowing up woodland creatures. At one point, it barrels through Paul Bartel's garden party, almost running over Mary Woronov. Predictably, and thankfully, Dick Miller is in here too.

Max (Kenneth McMillan) and Charlie (Randy Quaid) are the factory workers tasked with bringing the robots back before the vicious Crimebuster rolling tank destroys them. Max and Charlie realize that the robots have attained a form of sentience, and both men sympathize with the artificial beings. They later get help from Christopher Guest and Annie Potts, who play a pair of generous junkyard dealers.

Having taken almost instantly to domesticity, as Val and Aqua's batteries run down, they realize that "life" is about passing yourself along to another generation. They sacrifice

Jerry Garcia of the Grateful Dead provided Phil's voice.
(Copyright © Universal Pictures.)

their parts to keep Phil alive.

There's a happy ending, of course, being a PG movie from the '80s (Although, come to think of it, it was the very early '80s, which were still reeling from the anger and bad shoes of the '70s, so feel-good wasn't necessarily guaranteed), but the journey is low-key magical. The poignancy of the characters as they wind down is also sure to tug at the old decrepit heartstrings. We've been programmed to respond to beeps and pitch bends as emotional cues, and Phil has a wide vocabulary.

This was to be the feature film debut of avant-garde comedian Andy Kaufman. Originally, he and his partner, the equally strange Bob Zmuda, hoped to make a feature centered on their obnoxious alter ego, the unctuous lounge singer Tony Clifton, but studios weren't sure the *Taxi* star could carry a picture. So, they found something odd and seemingly safe. Robots were very in, what with the astronomical success of *Star Wars*.

Stan Winston was on board for the make-up effects. It seemed a no-brainer.

Kaufman wasn't thrilled. Arkush directs with an easy touch, but studios weren't happy with the "glacial" shooting pace. Kaufman would get bored and traipse off with Zmuda, who was officially banned from the set.

Winston's make-up is deceptively simple. The gaps between the translucent plastic holding Kaufman and Peters's expressions allow the actors to be at their most (strangely) subtly expressive.

For his part, Kaufman uses his "Foreign Man" character as the base for Val but veers into Judd Hirsch's New York accent. Both he and Peters are as lovely to watch as Shields and Yarnell's "Robot Breakfast" routine.

Taken on its own merits, *Heartbeeps* is charming rather than "unbearably coy," as Vincent Canby's dismissive review put it. Interestingly, largely because of Arkush's direction, the film feels very down to Earth despite taking place in the then-near, now-here-without-androids future. At times, it almost feels like a "this is what robots do in the wild" mini documentary. And that's not a bad thing.

The final cut "horrified" the studio—although what that word means, I've never been able to ascertain. Regardless, the studio cut it up to 79 lean minutes, making the sentience awakening a bit abrupt. The film opened and closed to little fanfare when it was dumped on audiences at Christmastime in 1981. (The *Rocky Horror* pseudo-sequel *Shock Treatment* was given similar respect in October, with Fox trying desperately to sell the latter movie as a horror film in many markets, which didn't work.) Arkush doesn't even like to talk about it.

But then there's *Get Crazy*.

If you like anarchic comedies that take place in their own reality, *Get Crazy* was made for you.

An anything-goes rock 'n' roll comedy, *Get Crazy* is set on New Year's Eve 1982 as the intrepid employees of the Saturn Theater prepare for their fifteenth annual rock concert. But an evil corporate mogul wants to tear the theater down to make way for a soulless mega-structure of his own. So, it's a race against time—can the heroes assemble the best line-up for their concert and raise enough money to buy the Saturn for themselves, or will corporate America prevail? The film stars Daniel Stern, Gail Edwards, Allen Garfield, and a gang of Corman regulars verses Ed Begley, Jr., Miles Chapin, Bobby Sherman, and Fabian (as the slimy execs in silver jumpsuits). The musical acts include Lou Reed, Lee Ving, Howard Kaylan, and Malcolm McDowell. There's also

Last Chance To Party This Summer!

Get Crazy

...And Say Goodbye To Your Brain!

a magical drug dealer named "Electric Larry" who keeps saving the day.

With a plot from the earliest episodes of *The Muppet Show* (or *The Little Rascals*, for that matter), *Get Crazy* is more of an insane celebration of rock 'n' roll theatrics and the love independents have for anything they consider their home.

Your enjoyment of *Get Crazy* improves with your rock 'n' roll knowledge, as there are music-related in-jokes stuffed in among the unrestrained sight gags (recreated album covers, characters named after drum solos, and many other things I'm way too unhip to get). And while it's tempting to describe the joke-per-second movie as "*Airplane*-inspired," Arkush's direction has a differently inspired tone. He tracks away from the setup-joke-setup-joke style of the Zucker Brothers and makes the

wonderful decision to instead just pack the frame with as much as lunacy as possible. The seven-foot-tall joint with a face that talks and is eventually smoked down to almost nothing is given no explanation, nor does it need one, and Arkush never dwells on it. Most of the gags are that fast and furious, ensuring that the viewer will watch *Get Crazy* over and over again to catch everything. (On my most recent viewing, I caught Ving's Piggy swiping a bra from a groupie who may be Linnea Quigley. I might be misplacing her; the shot is very quick, but I know she's in there somewhere.)

The most remarkable thing about *Get Crazy* is that it's a kitchen sink movie that was never meant to be kitchen sink. Arkush originally conceived the movie as a tribute to New York's Fillmore East, where he worked as an usher during his youth (Arkush's director's cameo in *Get Crazy* shows him wearing a Fillmore East T-shirt). "Everything in that movie is based on real stuff, and I wish I could remake it as a realistic movie. But the only way I could get it made at the time was to do the *Airplane!* version of it. My second film, *Heartbeeps* (1981), had been a complete failure, and I was desperate to do a movie about something I really knew and cared about."[1]

Arkush's biggest problem with the film came from the outset, during casting. Producer Herb Solow was

---

[1] "The Hollywood Interview" by Alex Simon and Terry Keefe. 2009. http://thehollywoodinterview. blogspot.com/2009/04/do-you-wanna-dance-allan-arkush.html

combative and dismissive of Arkush's ideas and intentions. What was meant to be a heartfelt *I Wanna Hold Your Hand* love letter to the Fillmore theaters became, under Solow, the *Airplane!* gagathon that we have (and I love) today. Arkush likens it to "3,000 punchlines but only 1,000 jokes." And while I love the casting that resulted, Arkush had wanted Tom Hanks (fresh from *Bosom Buddies* but before *Bachelor Party*), for instance.

"I've got to say this: Allen Garfield was the wrong choice. I'm sorry, I'm being completely honest," Arkush told *Exploitation Nation*'s Andrew J. Rausch. "He's a great actor, but I wanted Jerry Orbach, who was very much like [Fillmore owner] Bill Graham. He looked like him. And Bill Graham had been in show business, and Jerry Orbach had been in Broadway musicals. This is before *Law and Order*. That's who I had in mind. But they didn't want him, so we ended up with Allen Garfield, who is not a comedic actor. Thus, this kind of loose, comedic style I was going for didn't suit him."

On the other hand, Arkush was satisfied not only with the musical acts, but the performances the musicians gave. But the true star of the film is Malcolm McDowell, whose Reggie Wanker sends up and celebrates the Mick Jaggers and Rod Stewarts of the '70s.

"Malcolm was awesome," Arkush told Rausch. "Malcolm was hilarious. One of the great Malcolm moments was—we had already started shooting, and he came in late. He replaced someone. We go to a recording studio for him to record 'Hot Stuff,' and he's had the tracks, he's going along, and oh, it's awful! [*laughs*] *He can't sing at*

all! Again, it was a great spirit. We're in this together. Let's figure this out. Malcolm goes, 'How about I do it like a dramatic reading?' I go, 'Yeah, let's make it a little more like drama-pop!' That's why it is. He doesn't have to sing. He sort of shouts the words and says them dramatically, which is why when he sings 'Sadly' onstage, it's a little, uh…*pitchy*. He was fantastic. It was a joy to work with him."

Once Arkush leaned into the process and accepted that the movie he was making was…the movie he was making, at least the director's morale improved. "The chaos of making the movie was totally energizing, and the hero behind the movie—I'm going to give you this. I've never said this: The hero of *Get Crazy* is a guy by the name of Cliff Coleman. Cliff Coleman was the first AD. I needed the most hardcore punkers and crowds of people for most of the shoot, almost every day with New Year's Eve. I needed a really intense AD who was tremendously experienced with the scheduling of it, which was very difficult. We could only afford to do the movie if we didn't have Teamsters, and the only way we could not have Teamsters was to be in one location the entire time. You have Teamsters for errands, but you don't have trucks. That was a huge savings. But that made the schedule…everything had to be shot in the theater. Cliff was awesome. I chose Cliff because the movie he had done that I had seen was *The Wild Bunch* (1969). Get it? If you can do those shootouts, you can handle 500 hardcore punkers! Cliff infused it with this spirit.

"As it turns out, his father is C.C. Coleman, who was an AD for Frank

Borzage (director of *A Farewell to Arms* [1932]) for years. Cliff had started as a second AD. I found all this out later. If you're a film buff, Cliff's first job was— he replaced the second AD on the John Ford movie *Two Rode Together* (1961), with Jimmy Stewart and Richard Widmark. It's like a slightly different version of *The Searchers* (1956) but not as good.

"Cliff helped launch all that energy and all that background stuff, and he used to fire a blank pistol in the air to get everyone's attention."

In the end, the people responsible for financing *Get Crazy* never really understood the movie. Once the production was wrapped, a *Producers*-esque scheme was hatched to sell shares to a tax shelter group in the hopes that it would lose money. To wit, the film was thrown away.

Barely released by Embassy Pictures, *Get Crazy* was available for a while on VHS with an incorrect open-matte transfer that showed overhead booms and electrical equipment at the bottom of the screen. Since that format was added to the endangered species list, the film has failed to receive an official DVD release, one that may never emerge due to, according to Arkush, the disintegration of the original sound master tapes. Every now and then, a Blu-ray release is announced, but nothing concrete has emerged. There's a lovely copy circulating on streaming platforms, widescreen and stereo, that's worth catching when it comes around.

What the director dismisses as "too bizarre" and cluttered its many find delightful and brilliant. *Get Crazy* is anarchic, hilarious, destructive, and it utterly panders to youth and nostalgia. It's rock 'n' roll.

Ladies and Gentlemen: Electric Larry! (From Get Crazy. (Copyright © Embassy Pictures. All Rights Reserved.)

ARTS, PARTS, AND THE SAUCE OF DR. DUCK

BY TERRY THOME

During the second season of *The Monkees*, a discussion occurs between creators Bob Rafelson and Bert Schneider and the four leads—Micky Dolenz, Peter Tork, Davy Jones, and Michael Nesmith—over what direction the third season should take. Airing in 1966, the first season hedged its bet on its teenybopper audience by wedging itself between surf and British Invasion cultures. Yes, *The Monkees* was heavily influenced by The Beatles movie *A Hard Day's Night*, but The Monkees drove around in a muscle car (designed by Dean Jeffries) and lived seaside in a huge beach house. Even *The Monkees'* theme song was drenched in West Coast reverb.

By the second season, the four leads had begun to resent being just four hired hands in a huge multimedia project. They got all of the accolades and derision but had no control over their destiny. The group scored a major win when they wrested control over the show's musical direction from Don Kirshner. After that, they set their sights on the show itself. The 1966/1967 season became more freeform, with many fourth-wall breaks and an almost Dadaist surrealism that complemented the burgeoning psychedelic movement and brought it safely into American homes during prime time. The actors playing The Monkees actually became *The Monkees*.

For the third season, The Monkees wanted to take the show a completely different direction. They proposed a variety show format that would expand on their stream of consciousness leanings and include more pointed political humor and musical performances by scene groups and musicians. Those talks dissolved when the NBC network canceled the show outright. Rafelson and Schneider were done with the project anyway, both eager to move on to bigger, more "legitimate" things. Cannily, a year later, NBC premiered a variety show with topical comedy and musical performances from scene groups and musicians. That show was called *Laugh-In*.

After a TV special and a swan song movie, *Head*, the entire project involving The Monkees dissolved. The members of the group all went on to other projects. Tork went back to folk music, Jones became a reliable TV celebrity and pop singer, Dolenz did work behind and in front of the camera, and Nesmith went completely into country music with his First National Band. The First National Band's three albums, released by RCA in 1970/1971, were critical, though not financial, successes. The shadow of Monkee Mike was long, and it affected his solo output. A cult, however, was growing.

With help from his mother, Nesmith formed Pacific Arts in late 1974. The label concentrated on the types of music Nesmith championed—namely country and easy listening. The first release was an LP with accompanying book titled *The Prison*. The book was to be read in conjunction with the record as soundtrack. By most accounts, it didn't really work all that well, but it was adequately received as an interesting multimedia novelty.

In 1977, after buying his First National Band output from RCA, Nesmith recorded his first proper pop album, *From a Radio Engine to the Photon Wing*. The songs were generally less wistful than Nesmith's previous output and had a distinct tinge of island music. One of the songs from that album, "Rio," was chosen as a single by Pacific Arts international distributor Island Records. Island requested that Nesmith make a performance clip for the song to be played on overseas shows like *Top of the Pops*. This sort of practice was normal in the pop/rock world. Where an American artist was prohibited from doing a promotional tour overseas, said artist could make a film of a performance and send it out to many places around the world simultaneously. Nesmith, always a showman and forward-thinker,

decided to instead make a short film on his own dime.

Rio, directed by cinematographer/ director/collaborator Bill Dear, was a bright homage to the singing-and-dancing movies of the 1930s. The resulting film was a success in markets where it played and put "Rio" on the music charts there. However, in the United States, where the clip received virtually no play, "Rio" stiffed on the Billboard pop charts and only made the top 200.

Two years later, in 1979, Nesmith released his *Infinite Rider on the Big Dogma* LP. It was a full-on rock album designed to have a promo film for every track. The first song to be released with a promo clip was "Cruisin' (Lucy and Ramona and Sunset Sam)." "Cruisin'" was a quasi-proto-rap song about three SoCal drifters who cross paths and become soulmates. The video clip, directed by Bill Dear, visualized the lyrics of the song as a mini movie.

Thanks, in part, to the clip playing as a short between feature programming on Home Box Office (HBO), "Cruisin'" became a popular clip wherever it aired. Nesmith was emboldened and began pushing the idea of "music video" being the next step in the evolution of recorded music.

Nesmith and Dear then collaborated on a project titled *PopClips*, a half-hour program made up of music video clips hosted by various comedians. The show appeared on the Warner Amex cable channel, although only half of the taped episodes saw airtime. Nesmith, on the strength of the show, began pitching the idea of a channel devoted to music television; radio for the eyes, as it were. After many discussions over what the channel should consist of, Nesmith broke ties with Warner Amex, which proceeded on its own with the creation of MTV. At that time, Nesmith's mother had passed on, leaving him with a sizable fortune and future royalties on the Liquid Paper™ patent that had been the source of her wealth.

Nesmith, who, for years, had pontificated on the rise of "video albums," finally decided it was time to make one. It was to be a show filled with music videos and comedy skits, entitled *Elephant Parts*. The title refers to an old Far Eastern parable about a group of blind men who try to visualize what an elephant looks like by touching only one part of the animal. Of course, every man had a different idea of what the animal was in relation to what part of the elephant was touched. That, in Nesmith's oblique estimation, was what his video program was: a bunch of things that, on their own, seemed to be one thing, but became something else altogether in the bigger picture.

Elephant Parts was an hour-long variety show comprising Nesmith's music videos and comedy skits written and performed by Nez and a host of comedic writers and performers. Chief among those writers was humorist, satirist, and songwriter Bill Martin, whose most famous creation came with his story and screenplay *Harry and the Hendersons*, which Dear directed. Martin played a number of roles in *Elephant Parts*, including the Alphabet Pirate. Overall, the show's humor had a *Saturday Night Live* short-film feel, but more drug-oriented and much less scatalogical. In short, it was steeped in West Coast comedy.

The show included commercials for "Elvis Drugs," "art by the pound," and Nesmith's live LP, *Live at the Palais*, which could also make pasta and julienne fries. "Name That Drug," a game show spoof of *Name That Tune* in which a stoner (Martin) goes head-to-head with a narcotics officer (Nesmith) over who can identify a specific strand of marijuana, is both in the mold of Cheech and Chong and a harbinger of what the ABC TV show *Fridays* would bring to the table soon after.

The best bits are the ones using wordplay (or lack thereof). The "Bitty Soda" skit features Nesmith speaking in a gibberish form of the French language (The skit is also subtitled in gibberish). Meanwhile, the mariachi translator has Nez poorly translating the lyrics of a Spanish song to his date.

Musically, Nez brought his clips for "Rio" and "Cruisin'" on board, along with new clips from "Magic," "Light," and "Tonite," all from the *Infinite Rider on the Big Dogma* LP. The best musical moment comes at the very start, with Nesmith singing his First National Band hit "Joanne," but substituting the name of Toho kaiju star Rodan instead. The camera pans down to see Nesmith wearing monster-suit legs and trampling on a miniature town. This first scene is basically the manifesto of *Elephant Parts*. If you get this and it makes you double over, welcome, friend! You're in the right place.

The program premiered on VHS and Beta in June of 1981 for $59.95

as the world's first video album, with a laser disc edition coming the following year, priced at $39.95 (A "video 45" single was also released in 1983 through Sony Home Video, featuring the "Rio" and "Cruisin'" clips on VHS and Beta at a $29.95 price point). Nesmith's foresight paid off. The video was released right at the beginning of the home video boom, and an hour-long program that was not available on television or in theaters was enticing to early adopters of the formats.

By 1982, Nesmith had begun to turn his attention to theatrical features, beginning with *Timerider: The Adventure of Lyle Swann*. Released in early 1983, the film was not a success. At that time, Brandon Tartikoff (the head of programming at NBC) had approached Nesmith about creating a weekly prime-time series based on the *Elephant Parts* model. Nesmith was enthusiastic about the idea and delivered an hour-long pilot, *Television Parts*, to the network.

Television Parts picked up where *Elephant Parts* left off, but on a much larger scale thanks to the million-dollar budget afforded Nesmith by NBC. Nesmith was executive producer, while Ward Sylvester, the producer of *The Monkees* TV show, produced again. Suddenly, it began to look like the seeds of *The Monkees'* aborted season three were about to sprout on the same network, although nearly 20 years later.

Whether because of budget or the roster of expanded talent, *Television Parts* is a quantum leap over *Elephant Parts*. Whereas *Elephant Parts* was an edgier *SNL* not ready for prime-time production, *Television*

Parts was bigger, broader, and weirder than its counterpart. It was equal parts Ernie Kovacs, Monty Python, and Firesign Theatre. This is not to say it ever hit the heights of those giants, but the lineage is obvious. Nesmith himself hosted the show, addressing the audience like a New Age Will Rogers and pointing out the artifice of making television shows at every chance. Nesmith had a knack for finding comedic talent as well, using Whoopi Goldberg, Taylor Negron, Lois Bromfield, and Bob(cat) Goldthwait (whom Nesmith paid for out of pocket—NBC wanted nothing to do with him). *Television Parts* even made Jay Leno funny for a few moments.

The skits themselves are uniformly good, and a few of them (like Bromfield's "Sorority Girls from Hell" and Goldthwait's "Houdini the Pig") have taken on a mythic quality as shorts that everyone's "been looking for that for years," but no one could remember what it was from. There were also very short skits that you'd miss if you blinked. Five-second concerts mashed up popular tunes into musical punchlines ("Jaws the Knife," "There's No Business Like Star Wars"), while "Five-Second Theatre" did the same for classic films like *No Time for Sergeants* and the six-part miniseries *Thirty Seconds over Tokyo*). One particular recurring short, "Deep Thoughts by Jack Handy," later found much success as a recurring bit on *Saturday Night Live*.

Musically, *Television Parts* expanded on the *Elephant Parts* model by giving each song a large-scale production. Some of Nesmith's own songs became more whimsical ("Eldorado to the Moon," "I'll Remember You," etc.), while others ("Chow Mein and Bowling") showed Nez's affection for novelty tunes. Whereas Nesmith pretty much had the market cornered for music on *Elephant Parts* (undoubtedly out of necessity), a few popular artists contributed to *Television Parts*. Jimmy Buffet, Rosanne Cash, The Coyote Sisters, and Jim Stafford all had

95

featured musical guest spots on the show.

While the result seemed to please Tartikoff, the suits at NBC weren't at all convinced. Variety shows had fallen far from favor with television audiences. The last variety show NBC had was *Barbara Mandrell and the Mandrell Sisters*, and that had gone off the air in 1982. In the mid-1980s, the situation comedy reigned supreme, with simple plots that could be resolved by the half-hour mark. A viewer could leave the room, come back a few minutes later, and never miss a beat. *Television Parts* was ever-changing and freeform. It demanded viewers' absolute attention. Even a labored (and half-ironic) laugh track couldn't help to hold the attention of a *Cosby Show* fan.

The *Television Parts* pilot was sliced down to half an hour (with commercials). Test audiences were less than enthusiastic about it. The show finally aired in 1985 as part of NBCs legendary Thursday night "Must-See TV" lineup. It was pulled after one episode, revamped for a Friday night spot, and went largely unwatched then too. The remaining episodes were cut into a 90-minute one-off showing in the 11:30 *Saturday Night Live* time slot, again to little fanfare.

Undaunted, Nesmith took his baby back to where it began. Two concurrent home video programs were made from the many skits and musical performances: *Television Parts Home Companion*, which focused largely on Nesmith-related music and comedy material, and *Dr. Duck's Super Secret All-Purpose Sauce*, which consisted largely of the non-Nesmith comedy skits. While neither program gathered the attention that *Elephant Parts* did, both releases were met with a faithful cult audience.

In the years that followed, Nesmith released these videos in various forms, including a late '90s double laser disc pairing *Elephant Parts* with his then-current *Live at the Britt Festival*. Also included is a collection of Nesmith's music videos from various programs, entitled *Nezmusic*, which was released in conjunction with the CD compilation *The Newer Stuff*. The videos from *Elephant Parts* were released on DVD in 2012 as a part of the UK Edsel Records CD boxset *The Pacific Arts Box*. *Elephant Parts* was given a DVD release in 1998 as a special "17 ½ Anniversary Edition" from DVD International. It was then released again in 2003 by Anchor Bay Entertainment, complete with a new commentary track featuring Nesmith discussing the making of *Elephant Parts*. The latter release improved upon the first LD commentary track, which featured Nez in full evasive, abstruse mode.

Neither *Television Parts* nor *Dr. Duck's* have had a digital physical media rerelease, but the original programs are still available on VHS from Nesmith himself through his Videoranch website.

For the new millennium, Papa Nez's Videoranch channel on YouTube features every segment from *Elephant Parts*, *Television Parts*, and *Dr. Duck* uploaded as individual video clips. The clips have been curated into different playlists if you want to see what they were like as released, but the channel also provides you the opportunity to create your own "Dr. Parts" compilation.

THE 'BURBS (1989)

BY MIKE WATT

The 'Burbs is a black comedy directed by Joe Dante and starring Tom Hanks, Carrie Fisher, Corey Feldman, Henry Gibson, and Dick Miller. It also features Brother Theodore as "Reuben Klopek."

Born Theodore Isidore Gottlieb, Brother Theodore was a comedian in much the same way SIDS is a relief from the high cost of childcare. What he practiced as an artform was something he called "stand-up tragedy."

Born into a wealthy German family, Gottleib was imprisoned in Dachau. There, he signed over his family fortune for a single Reichsmark to secure his freedom. Later, he was expelled from Switzerland for "chess hustling."

"I gazed into the abyss, and the abyss gazed into me, and *neither of us* liked what we saw!"

Brother Theodore had a bit part in Orson Welles's 1946 film *The Stranger*. From that moment on, he seemed to remain in black and white for the rest of his life (except when he was in *The*

Brother Theodore IS Uncle Reuben Klopek in The 'Burbs. With Tom Hanks (left).

'Burbs—that was in color).

"All of our moral leaders are dead!" he proclaimed. "Moses is dead! Mohammed is dead! And I don't feel so hot myself!"

Dubbed "a genius of the sinister," Brother Theodore performed for years in a one-man show in which he sat at a table beneath a bare light and screamed at the audience in his thick German accent, scaring many of them so badly that they came back the next night. Of course, Germans sound angry when they say, "I love you." Their language lacks an inside voice.

"The moment anyone is born, they are doomed! Life has a 100 percent mortality rate!" He also said, "When I die, I want my head severed from my body and replaced with a bouquet of broccoli. It's the artist in me."

Most people my age remember the Rankin and Bass animated *The Hobbit* when it ran on TV 9n 1977. Brother Theodore gave voice to Gollum, and while his Gollum was no Andy Serkis, Serkis isn't any kind of Brother Theodore. This is unassailable logic.

"As long as there is death, there is hope!"

Always feeling like he was on the verge of a great career, Brother Theodore was often a victim of his own self-sabotage. Despite appearing in a semi-porn version of *Jaws* called *Gums* (1976), his great career never really took off. Though he was a frequent and beloved guest on *The Tonight Show* (and less beloved on *David*

Letterman—most of his segments with Dave, he'd painstakingly scripted beforehand, and Letterman really sold the idea that Theodore wandered in and demanded attention), his name was far from household usage.

Theodore made *The 'Burbs* in 1989. He died in 2001. I don't think *The 'Burbs* can be blamed.

If you want to know more about Brother Theodore, there's a terrific documentary about him called *To My Great Chagrin: The Unbelievable Story of Brother Theodore* (2008), by Jeff Sumerel, edited by Jeter Rhodes, and it's highly entertaining.

The 'Burbs is available on DVD too. I think I mentioned that Tom Hanks is in it too, but he made that before he became important.

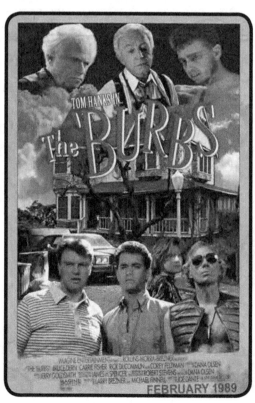

MATT HELM AND DEAN MARTIN

BY MIKE HAUSHALTER

In the late '60s, the three B's ruled the universe: The Beatles, Batman, and Bond, James Bond. Film producer Irving Allen (much like Dick Rowe from Decca Records) had almost been in on the James Bond phenomenon in 1959, back when he was a production partner with Albert "Cubby" Broccoli. But some unkind words from Allen about the Bond novels spoiled the deal, and it would take a few more years for Bond to reach movie screens (with no involvement from Allen). In 1964, as James Bond fever was burning around the world, Allen decided he wanted in on some of that sweet spy swag he had missed out on. After reading one of Donald Hamilton's *Matt Helm* novels at an airport, Allen decided that Matt Helm would be the perfect character to build an American "Bond" franchise, and he quickly purchased the rights. In retrospect, Hamilton's series was the perfect property to compete with Bond. Many fans and critics at the time already considered Matt Helm the American James Bond, a character just as tough and resourceful as his literary "cousin" across the sea.

In a bid to go head to head with the Bond outings as serious competitors, the film series started out as a straightforward spy thriller, with Paul Newman expected to star. This did not come to fruition, as no one at the time really wanted to go up against Connery or be tied down by a four- or five-picture deal. Instead, it was decided that the series would take the comedy route and the films would be parodies of the genre. Dean Martin was called upon to portray Matt Helm. He certainly had it in him to turn Helm into a great character and give Bond a run for his money, but unfortunately, he didn't even really try. I am not saying he does a bad job as Helm, only that he and the script turned the cynical antihero that Helm embodied into pretty much just a hard-boiled (or is that pickled?) version of Martin's boozy lounge singer persona. This makes for OK viewing but is a big letdown to most anyone who has read the books.

***The Silencers* (1966).** BIG O, a third-rate SPECTRE-wannabe led by Tung-Tze (Victor Buono), is planning on sabotaging America's nuclear arms program and flooding half the country

with radioactive waste. America's top spy agency, ICE (Intelligence and Counter-Espionage), is on BIG O's trail. Unfortunately, ICE's only real hope of stopping BIG O, its top agent, Matt Helm, has retired. ICE must get Helm to give up retirement, including his new day job as a photographer for *Slaymate* magazine, and thwart BIG O before it is too late.

The Silencers is a jaunty pastiche of James Bond and the Swinging Sixties that stars the king of cool himself, Dean Martin, as laid-back, booze-swilling hero Matt Helm.

The film starts off with a bang (and a bump and grind) with a trio of eye-catching, ooh la la burlesque numbers, and the film's theme song is sung by Vikki Carr and lip-synched by Cyd Charisse. *The Silencers* has some decent action scenes, some car crack-ups, fisticuffs and even a few cool gadgets (hand grenade coat buttons, a knife-launching camera, and a

trick gun that never shoots where you think it will). The film also has a surprisingly strong cast that includes James Gregory as the head of faux spy agency ICE; Beverly Adams as Helm's personal secretary, Lovey Kravezit; Stella Stevens as the good girl, Daliah Lavi; and Nancy Kovack as another requisite femme fatale. Robert Webber and Roger C. Carmel also star as tough-talking henchman, while Victor Buono plays the head baddie.

As '60s spy films go, *The Silencers* is fairly above average. It is a mostly fun romp (a bit cringey by today's more enlightened times, mind you) that is chock-full of pin-up girl eye candy and has a bit of a Adam West *Batman* feel. Due to its broad humor and low budget, the film doesn't really compare well to the Bond films of the time (or of any time), but it's better than many of the Euro-spy films of the time. Surprisingly, the film does recreate several bits from Hamilton's novels *Death of a Citizen* and *The Silencers*.

***Murderers' Row* (1966).** Super hip superspy Matt Helm travels to France to track down and rescue Dr. Solaris, a missing laser-weapons inventor who has been kidnapped by the nefarious BIG O.

A scant 10 months after the release of *The Silencers*, hard-drinking, wise-cracking Dean Martin strapped on his flask and picked up a martini to once again become playboy photographer/superspy Matt Helm for the follow-up film, *Murderers' Row*. Arriving just in time for the Christmas holiday, *Murderers' Row* is another breezy tale of world-saving and booze-drinking that's full of beautiful women, keen gadgets, and boffo locations that probably inspired *Austin Powers* just as much as *You Only Live Twice*. Though the second installment did not do as much box office as its predecessor, to me, it's the better film and seems just a bit more polished.

For one thing, *Murderers' Row* probably has the best cast of the series (or perhaps it just makes the best use of its cast). The lineup includes Dean Martin, who again shows why he was known as the king of cool and plays himself to the hilt; megastar sex kitten Ann-Margret, dancing her heart out and looking out of this world in posh costumes; and slumming legend Karl Malden as head baddie Julian Wall. They are backed up by the returning James Gregory as Helm's boss and Beverly Adams as Helm's personal assistant. Some new faces include Camilla Sparv (*Dead Heat on a Merry-*

CAMILLA SPARV · JAMES GREGORY · BEVERLY ADAMS

Introducing DINO, DESI and BILLY · Featuring the "Slaygirls" · Screenplay by HERBERT BAKER
Based on the novel by DONALD HAMILTON · Music by Lalo Schifrin · Produced by IRVING ALLEN
Directed by HENRY LEVIN · A Meadway-Claude Picture TECHNICOLOR

Go-Round) as bad girl Coco Duquette and Tom Reese (*Vanishing Point*) as Ironhead, an actual threatening henchman, strait out of the Oddjob/ Jaws school of heavies, who provides some decent menace.

The film also features a decent car chase, a shaken-not-stirred death trap, a bang-up pyrotechnic-filled hovercraft chase, and a trick pistol with a 7-second delay that proves its worth in the frenzied climax.

On the minus side, the dialogue is dated, the effects are cheesy, and Martin and Ann-Margret have almost zero chemistry. It's like they are two super powerful magnets that attract everything but each other.

A third installment, *The Ambushers*, would arrive just in time for Christmas 1967.

The Ambushers (1967). Helm (still Dean Martin) travels to Acapulco, where he clashes with foreign spies, BIG O, and the exiled ruler of a rogue nation in a race to obtain a hijacked experimental flying saucer belonging to the U.S. government.

I imagine I probably watched all of the Matt Helm films half a dozen times or more on television when I was growing up. Unlike the Bond films, the Helm films were often played as the afternoon movie. Much like the hallowed "*Plant of the Apes* Week," all four Helm films would occasionally be shown in a row with plenty of fanfare and ballyhoo to ensure that young scamps like me would be sitting in front of the tube rather than outside in the sunshine. For one reason or another, *The Ambushers* has always been the Helm film that sticks with me the most. Perhaps this is because it's the one with the UFO, telekinetic ray pistols, and army of sexy Slaygirls. Perhaps I just saw it the most times. Either way, it's my favorite.

Beyond my fond recollections, I now also appreciate the film for being a bit more faithful to its paperback source material (even if only in spirit in some cases). The script lifts several scenes, bits of dialogue, and an important McGuffin from the novel. In addition, head villain Jose Ortega (Albert Salmi) is much more in line with the antagonists Helm faces in the books. Ortega is also far more perverse and menacing than any of the other cinematic Helm villains, who, for the most part, are camp caricatures at best.

The icing on the cake for me is femme fatale Francesca Medeiros, played by a super gorgeous Senta Berger. Berger comes very close to bringing one of my favorite characters from the Helm novels, Vadya, to life, albeit with a different name. In the books, Vadya is a Russian agent who forms an uneasy alliance with Helm. The same happens in the film with

Dean Martin and Senta Berger in The Ambushers. (Copyright © Columbia Pictures. All Rights Reserved.)

Francesca, only she works for BIG O instead of Mother Russia.

Like the other films in the series, *The Ambushers* has a fine cast. Martin is at his series best showing off his charm and a bit of his acting ability. Gregory and Adams show up for the last time as Helm's boss and personal secretary, respectively. Janice Rule plays the almost age-appropriate love interest and UFO pilot Sheila Sommers. In addition to the already mentioned Berger and Salmi, the marvelous Kurt Kasznar plays beer-brewing villain Quintana. The cast is also joined by a bevy of beautiful Slaygirls.

The film boasts a fantastic soundtrack courtesy of Hugo Montenegro, including a catchy theme song (minus some cringey lyrics). There are also tons of cool gadgets, such as the aforementioned UFO, ray guns, bullet-firing bras, laughing-gas cigarettes, and knockout lipstick.

All in all, *The Ambushers* is a top-of-the-line James Bond knockoff.

The Wrecking Crew **(1968).** ICE sends their top agent, Matt Helm (Dean Martin), to Copenhagen to thwart plans hatched by criminal mastermind Count Massimo Contini (Nigel Green) to collapse the economy of the free world by stealing $1 billion in gold bullion. When Helm arrives in Denmark, he has to deal with a trio of sexy femme fatales out to kill him (Lola Medina [Tina Louise], Linka Karensky [Elke Sommer], and Yu-Rang [Nancy Kwan]). He must also contend with Freya Carlson (Sharon Tate), a beautiful but bungling woman from the Danish tourism bureau who has been assigned to help Helm but who usually causes more problems than she fixes.

Thanks to Quentin Tarantino's *Once Upon a Time in Hollywood*, *The Wrecking Crew* is now probably the best-known of Martin's four Matt Helm outings. This is kind of a shame, as almost anyone getting their first taste of a Helm film with *The Wrecking Crew* will probably not go on to check out any of the other films.

Sorry to say, but *The Wrecking Crew* is a very tired and listless film from a series that, at its best, was just above average.

Even as a fan of the series, I have a hard time recommending this one. The movie has nothing at all to do with the fantastic paperback namesake. It's silly, racist, sexist, and just overall underwhelming. It's a bloated wreck of a film that wastes a ton of talent both on and off screen. Onscreen, the likes of Louise (*Gilligan's Island*), Sommer (*A Shot in the Dark*), and Green (*The Ipcress File*) sleepwalk their way to a paycheck, leaving only Tate (*Valley of the Dolls*) and Kwan (*Wonder Women*) to actually care. Top dog Martin fails hardest, giving the film nearly less effort than he put in for *The Dean Martin Show*. At times, *The Wrecking Crew* almost seems like a skit from said show more than a film. It's also the first film to have an onscreen appearance by Chuck Norris, but he contributes nothing more than a trivia answer. Behind the scenes, the man, the myth, the legend Bruce Lee toiled to make Kwan and Tate look like they could fight, and mighty martial artist Mike Stone doubled Martin's fight scenes (to make him look like he could fight),

but Lee and Stone's hard work didn't seem to make much of a difference in the finished product.

The film's end credits promised a fifth installment to be called *The Ravagers*, and a crossover with Frank Sinatra's Tony Rome films was also hinted at in the trades, but sadly, neither of these efforts came to be. Whether it was Tate's tragic death, the law of diminishing returns, or just Martin being tired of playing the part, *The Wrecking Crew* put an end to the Matt Helm films.

The character was resurrected in 1975 on a TV show, with Anthony Franciosa playing Helm as a former spy turned PI. The show lasted a season and had even less to do with the source novels than Martin's films. Rumors of a reboot have been kicked around for years, but I highly doubt another Helm will ever see the light of day.

THE WRONG GUY
OR
"IT ISN'T CITIZEN KANE"

BY JASON LANE

Writing articles like these, I do my best to remain objective. With honest eyes, I look at films I don't like and evaluate what the filmmakers were trying to, did accomplish, and failed to achieve. But every once in a while, I get a film like *The Wrong Guy*.

I love this goddamn movie.

It's slightly off-kilter, just enough to where you wonder if the writers included jokes that they themselves liked more so than, say, the general public, which meant that it would be adored by critics more so than, say, the general public.

This is a nice way of saying the movie didn't do very well.

After discovering *The Wrong Guy* much later than I should have (I just watched the damn thing two years ago!), I immediately fell in love with it. I liked how they took the tired premise of a chase movie and turned it on its head. It's not a deep movie; there's no underlying message about honesty, liberty, blah-blah. There's just a constant string of silly and stupid getting thrown at the camera in the hopes that something

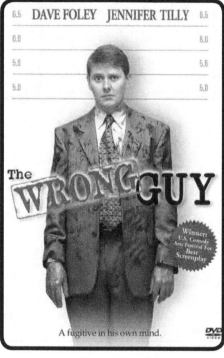

will stick. Well, good news, everybody! It do! It do! Well…mostly.

After watching the film a third time, I did a little reading on it for some behind-the-scenes info, and guess what? There wasn't much. However, I noticed something when I checked for the trailer on YouTube: The entire movie was there, free for anyone to watch. Not only that, but Dave Foley, the film's lead actor and writer, had written a message in the YouTube comments, saying that the movie was "something (he's) extremely proud of," he "wish(ed) more people had seen it," and he was "delighted that it has pleased some of you."

That may sound like something incredibly nice and sweet to say, but it's not that impressive. He's Canadian. You know how they are.

THE CHASE

The plot of the movie is straightforward enough. Foley plays Nelson Hibbert, an executive lined up to become the next president of Nagel Industries, the company for which he's toiled many a year. He's not getting promoted for his hard work and diligence as much as he's marrying the boss's daughter. He's also amazingly annoying and outright despised by everyone in the high-rise building, so he has that going for him. Even though Nelson has been waiting for years for the opportunity, since no one respects him or his work, including his boss, someone else is picked for the promotion. He doesn't take the news very well.

After going to his office and wailing like a lost banshee, he gains the strength to confront his future father-in-law. He barges into Mr. Nagel's office and lets him have it, telling him everything that's been

on his chest for the last decade or so. He then notices that Mr. Nagel isn't responding in the slightest. Nelson sees a bloody knife on the floor, picks it up, and then notices that his father-in-law has been murdered. After a minute of slow realization, Nelson figures out that, yes, the knife is the murder weapon, and yes, his fingerprints are all over it now!

Covered in blood, Nelson leaves the office with the knowledge that the last words people heard was him threatening to kill his boss. He leaves the building knowing that he has been framed, would not last a day in prison, and needs to get out of the country as fast as possible before police come to drag him away.

But the police aren't coming.

When the police arrive, they find a video showing a hitman killing the boss and Nelson stumbling onto the crime scene. They now have no interest in him since they know he's completely innocent; they merely want to talk to him to get a statement. Meanwhile, Nelson throws away his driver's license and credit cards as he tries to make it to the safety and the stability of...

105

wherever he's going. It's obvious that Nelson doesn't plan anything out more than one step in front of him. So, his main goal is to escape from the mecca of, uh, Cleveland and go anyplace that can keep him safe. With that, we're now following the desperate adventures of possibly the stupidest man alive. The film has a lot of fun with the fugitive trope, and it also smartly places some talented character actors where they can do good work. The hitman is something out of a James Bond movie (well, maybe the Roger Moore ones).

Likewise, the police are wonderfully inept. David Anthony Higgins stands out as Detective Arlen, a man armed with only his wits and an unchecked police credit card. He's greatly reminiscent of John Candy's Burton Mercer ("Orange whip? Orange whip?"), the parole officer assisting the cops in apprehending the Blues Brothers, and that is high praise indeed. The extraordinarily adorable Jennifer Tilly pops ups as a kind-of love interest and gets to do some physical comedy rather than just the ditzy role that, honestly, she's perfected. The series of scenes that happens after Nelson goes on the run is, at best, silly and, at worst, bizarre, but it works more often than not.

Those scruffy, rag-tag Canadians, the Kids in the Hall (L-R) Scott Thompson, Bruce McCollough, Mark McKinney, Dave Foley, Kevin McDonald. (Copyright © The Kids in the Hall. All Rights Reserved)

IT'S A FACT

The actors and their roles are listed below. See if you can count all the Canadians. (Spoiler alert: There are a bunch o' those polite bastards.) Whoa, Nelly, but this movie is Canadian as hell—er, I mean heck.

• **Dave Foley** as the annoying-to-everyone-but-himself protagonist Nelson Hibbert: Foley cofounded the elite-level comedy sketch group The Kids in the Hall (which is enough pedigree for anyone, but let's continue). He and fellow Canadian Phil Hartman also headed the sitcom *NewsRadio*. Foley has done tons of voiceover bits and memorable roles, including a standout part as All-American Boy, the sidekick teacher in *Sky High*. He also starred with his fellow Kids in the Hall in the criminally underrated film *Kids in the Hall: Brain Candy* and the criminally ignored miniseries *Kids in the Hall: Death Comes to Town*. Lotsa criminally ignored stuff here is what I'm sayin'.

- **Jennifer Tilly** as the sweetly innocent yet clumsily dangerous Lynn Holden: Husky-voiced and always adorable, Tilly is versatile as hell, navigating from drama to comedy with no trouble. In addition to her lengthy acting résumé, Tilly is probably most famous for two things: being a World Series of Poker winner and playing Tiffany Valentine, Chucky's female counterpart in the *Child's Play* movies. She also received an Academy Award nomination for her performance in Woody Allen's *Bullets over Broadway*, so make that three things for which she's probably known. World Series of Poker, *Bride of Chucky*—oh, wait, she's also the voice of Bonnie, the better half of the handicapable Joe Swanson on *Family Guy*. Let's just stop at four things.

- **David Anthony Higgins** playing Detective Arlen, who has little trouble playing a hunch no matter how expensive it is: Higgins is one of those actors who has a lot of roles on his résumé, but you know damn well that he needs to be a regular on a quality show. I mean, if those mannequins on *The Big Bang Theory* made all that money...? Anyway, Higgins is probably best known for his role as Craig Feldspar on *Malcolm in the Middle*, but he has appeared in *NewsRadio*, *Ellen*, *Mike and Molly*, *American Horror Story: Murder House*, *Mom*, and *Last Man Standing*. He also helped cowrite *The Wrong Guy*.

- **Kenneth Welsh** as Mr. Nagel, president of Nagel Industries and all-around bastard: Welsh is a Canadian character actor with a Brian Cox/Charles Durning appeal, and that is high praise. He has a lengthy list of acting credits under his belt, the most famous likely being the villainous Windom Earle on *Twin Peaks*. Welsh also has memorable bits in *Timecop*, *Legends of the Fall*, *The Exorcism of Emily Rose*, and the underrated horror gem *The Void*.

Canadian Flag. Copyright © Canada. All Rights Reserved, eh?

• **Dan Redican** as the job-stealing bastard Ken Daly: Redican is a Canadian and comedy veteran whose résumé includes writing, performing, and puppeteering work (yes, puppeteering). Best known for being a founding member of the Canadian comedy group The Frantics, Redican has worked regularly with the Jim Henson Company, the super-Canadian show *Corner Gas*, the ultra-Canadian shows *The Kids in the Hall* and *Kids in the Hall: Death Comes to Town*, the mega-Canadian show *Little Mosque on the Prairie*, and *Due South*(!). He may be the most Canadian man in this list.

• **Colm Feore** playing the Killer, a much better-than-he-needs-to-be assassin: Another damn Canadian, this actor is all over the place, with performances in *Thor*, *Thirty-Two Short Films about Glenn Gould* (He played Glenn Gould!), the award-winning *Trudeau*, *The West Wing*, *House of Cards*, *Face/Off*, *Storm of the Century*

(He played the evil dude that brought the storm!), *The Exorcism of Emily Rose*, and *The Changeling*. Also, to prove that he's totally paid his dues, Feore has appeared in shows like *Friday the 13th: The Series*, *War of the Worlds*, *Forever Knight*, and *Kung Fu: The Legend Continues*. Yeah, he's earned his props. He's now most famous with the young'uns for playing Sir Reginald Hargreeves/Monocle in *The Umbrella Academy*.

• **Joe Flaherty** playing Fred Holden, Lynn's always-exasperated father: Speaking of pedigrees, this man has one of the best. Flaherty was a writer and regular on legendary Canadian sketch-comedy show *SCTV*. His career is littered with memorable bit parts, including Sid Sleaze in *Sesame Street Presents: Follow That Bird*, the total dick who jeered Happy ("Jackass!") in *Happy Gilmore*, the freshly divorced and newly enraged dentist on *Married...with Children*, and Harold Weir on *Freaks and Geeks*. Most important to my nerdier friends out there, Flaherty was the Western Union man with the 70-year-old letter in *Back to the Future Part II*. Sidenote: His Count Floyd character was one of the best reoccurring characters on any sketch show ever. "OooooooOOOoooo! Spoooooooky, kids!" Biggest shock here? He's American (and not just American—Flaherty is from Pittsburgh! We claim this one!). Go, team!

• **Enrico Colantoni** as Creepy Guy: I don't really have much more to add to this. Guess what? He's Canadian, as well as being one of those chameleon actors who can

SCTV's Joe Flaherty as Count Floyd!
Not pictured: Canadians.

play any damn part he wants with no problem. Hero, villain, comedy, drama—he does it all and makes it look easy. He appeared on *Friday the 13th: The Series* and *3rd Rock from the Sun*. He was also Elliot the photographer on *Just Shoot Me!*; Keith Mars, the father on *Veronica Mars*; the main badass SWAT guy on *Flashpoint*; and the brilliant but lethal Carl Elias on the sadly underappreciated *Person of Interest*. However, Colantoni is easily best remembered as the aggressively meek alien Mathesar in *Galaxy Quest* (one of the best *Star Trek* movies ever).

• **Barenaked Ladies**, the best folk-rap band to listen to if Ben Folds or Dave Matthews Band is a little too edgy: The band makes a cameo as singing policemen who do an acceptable but overly long acapella song, "Gangster Girl." The band is most famous for dropping the super catchy song "One Week" on an unsuspecting populace in 1998. In case you couldn't escape Barenaked Ladies quickly enough, the band also did the theme song for *The Big Bang Theory*. They're Canadian too, but that should be no surprise. They aren't my favorites, but no less a superstar than Paul McCartney was quoted in 2008 as saying that they were better than he and John Lennon ever were and that he wouldn't mind recording with them in the future. (I merely stared out the window upon reading that, waiting for someone to tell me that I was in an alternate dimension or a coma or something. I dunno.)

The movie is littered with other great character actors who deserve a mention, but guess what? Life ain't fair. Just trust me when I say there are few weak links in this chain.

"THESE ARE THE DAVES I KNOW"

Movie: *The Wrong Guy*
Running time: *1 hr 32 min*
Country: *Canada (Duh!)*
Release date: *August 1st, 1997*
Written by: *Dave Foley,*
 David A. Higgins,
 Jay Kogen
Directed by: *David Steinberg*
Produced by: *Janet E. Cuddy,*
 Martin Walters,
 Jon Slan
Cinematography: *David A. Makin*
Music: *Lawrence Shragge*
Sound Mixing: *Dolby Digital*
Edited by: *Christopher Cooper*
Distributed by: *Lions Gate*
 Entertainment
Language: *Canadian (All right,*
 English. Ok?)
Available: *DVD, Blu Ray*
Awards: *US Comedy Arts Festival:*
 Best Screenplay (winner)

There is a lot to unpack here, so here we go. I've already talked about Foley and Higgins, but I haven't mentioned the other writer, Jay Kogen. Kogen has an extensive comedy background, producing and writing for series like *The Tracey Ullman Show*, *The Simpsons*, *Frasier*, *Everybody Loves Raymond*, and *Malcolm in the Middle*, but to me, he's a hero for acting on *It's Garry Shandling's Show* (which had one of the best theme songs ever). He's been nominated for *and* has won a bunch of Emmys too, usually for Outstanding Writing.

Director David Steinberg

was born in, wait for it, Canada. He's another comedy veteran with a long career in making people laugh. Some career highlights include guest-hosting *The Tonight Show* for Johnny Carson several times and working on shows like *The Smothers Brothers Comedy Hour*, *Newhart*, *The Golden Girls*, *Designing Women*, *It's Garry Shandling's Show* (!), *Seinfeld*, *Mad about You*, *Friends*, *Curb Your Enthusiasm*, and several of the actual Academy Awards shows. Actually, he's worked on so many Academy Awards shows that you'd think they'd just give him one, but whatever. He's received several Emmy nominations and managed to even win a couple of them.

I couldn't find anything other than professional history for producer Janet E. Cuddy, but I'd bet a shiny new quarter that she's Canadian. I also couldn't find anything she's done past 1999, so I hope she's OK. Her production history is wonderfully eclectic, with notable titles like *F/X2*, *Forever Knight*, *The Care Bears Movie*, *Videodrome*, and *Visiting Hours*.

Martin Walters has a distinguished career in cinema, usually as an assistant director. He's worked as an AD on films like *Watchmen*, *300*, *Diary of the Dead*, *Land of the Dead*, *Billy Madison*, *PCU*, and the Lifetime channel prototype movie, *The Cutting Edge*. I have no idea if he's Canadian.

Next up is…yep…Canada's own Jon Slan, who has produced some wicked awesome stuff, such as *Wyatt Earp*, *Forever Knight* (I'm seeing a pattern here), and *Lock, Stock, and Two Smoking Barrels*.

Cinematographer David A. Makin has been doing this for years, with *Schitt's Creek*, the *Tenacious D* series, *MADtv*, *Kids in the Hall: Brain Candy*, and *The Kids in the Hall* (series) as works of note.

Composer Lawrence Shragge has scored more than 180 films, so the dude must be doing something right.

Christopher Cooper has edited tons o' stuff, but he probably went the Makin route, as he also worked on *The Kids in the Hall*.

So, yeah, a lot of talented mofos worked on this film, and you can tell, as all of the shots and scenes work, if maybe not all of the jokes.

SLIPPED MY MIND

In 1997, the cinematic landscape was filled with overblown, high-budget spectacles. *Titanic, Men in Black*, and *The Lost World: Jurassic Park* led the pack with a combined worldwide gross of $3 billion. *The Full Monty* kept the hopes of low-budget filmmakers alive, costing $3.5 million to make and earning $255 million at the box office.

Comedies weren't in too much demand, though that year produced *Liar, Liar; Waiting for Guffman; Private Parts; Chasing Amy;* the not-talked-about-enough *Grosse Pointe Blank;* the talked-about-too-damn-much *Austin Powers: International Man of Mystery; The House of Yes* (where Parker Posey shows you how to act deliciously); *Bean; The Man Who Knew Too Little;* and the life-changing and multi-award-winning masterpiece *Good Burger*.

The Wrong Guy was released and, being Canadian, didn't make any fuss or noise. The only thing I noticed that could possibly have a "Look at me!" appeal was that when the movie came out, the poster showed Foley standing by himself with a deer-in-headlights look in front of a police lineup. A little while later, this image was replaced with a similar one showing other guys standing near Foley, the poster now looking very similar to the one for the just-released *The Usual Suspects*. But as such, *The Wrong Guy* quietly did its job and went back home, which is a shame because it should have achieved a cult status much sooner than it did.

It achieved that status a few months back, apparently.

I'm not sure how up you, dear reader, are on current events. Long story short, there is this shiny, brand-new superflu called COVID-19 that's specifically designed to f**k people up. In addition to being highly contagious, it's a double-threat to the obese, the elderly, and anyone with a compromised system. So, the best way to stop this is to limit interpersonal interactions, stay at home as much as possible, and easiest of all, wear a 1 oz. mask on your face for a small amount of time. The entire world was like, "Sure. If this will save people and get this thing over with, we'll do it."

But then there are these people called Americans, and you can't tell us shit. Oh, sure, 95 percent of the American population is wearing masks, practicing self-quarantining, etc. But man, that leftover 5 percent is not going to let something like saving people's lives interfere with their freedoms, so because of these freedom-touting patriots who love this country more than you and I will ever dream, we'll be done with this little annoyance around 2027.

Probably in the fall. Maybe.

Anyway, people are staying home more, so we're watching a lot more TV and movies than normal. I'm seeing almost a throwback to the days when word-of-mouth sold a movie better than reviews by Siskel and Ebert (although those reviews were very good). A constant crush of new Hollywood offerings and the availability of TV series on Amazon Prime/Netflix/Hulu/whatever for binge-watching afforded little chance for older films to get any notice. But with that pesky little lethal flu not only keeping people at home, but also severely decimating new film and television productions, people began to look at older fare. Some films that haven't been mentioned in a while have been brought up recently. Who brought them up? I did. "Some films" include the following. I've even included any show or musical group that inspired the movie, all for no extra charge!

Strange Brew, inspired by *SCTV*

Run, Ronnie, Run, inspired by *Mr. Show*

The Onion Movie, inspired by *The Onion* website

Reno 911: The Movie and *The Baxter*, inspired by *The State*

Forbidden Zone, inspired by The Mystic Knights of the Oingo Boingo

With all these names being tossed around, someone brought up *The Wrong Guy*. I said I'd neither seen it nor heard of it. Then, the words "one of the guys from *Kids in the Hall*" spilled out. I was instantly hooked, but

"This is a knife! THIS is a knife! This IS a knife!" (Copyright © Lions Gate Entertainment. All Rights Reserved.)

I steeled myself, as there are dozens of examples where someone from a sketch show can't translate that success to the silver screen (and no, I'm not talking specifically about Chevy Chase). Anyway, I hunted the movie down (As previously mentioned, I looked up the trailer on YouTube and found the entire movie available to watch for free) and watched it. And I loved it.

THINGS WE COULDN'T SHOW

The Wrong Guy is just a stupidly fun movie. The actors jump into their parts with relish and look to be having a great time while doing so. The movie does the standard odd guy/gorgeous lady trope with reasonable explanation (She's juuuuuust a leetle bit flawed). It always irritated me when some goofy-looking guy gets the beautiful girl in the film, like Seth Rogan and Katherine Heigl in Knocked Up, Chevy Chase and Goldie Hawn in Seems Like Old Times, and every one

of Adam Sandler's movies. The only flaw I can find is that in the beginning, Foley, à la Jay Sherman in The Critic or Kenny Powers in the HBO series Eastbound and Down, dares to make his Nelson Hibbert unlikeable to the audience. But unlike Jay and Kenny, Nelson is a genuinely nice guy, if a bit of a dumbass, so a sympathetic side does eventually come out. Also, since this movie is wholly Canadian, there's very little violence, cursing, or sex. That would just be rude. Eh, buddy?

So, all of this blah-blah boils down to the following: If you like goofy comedies, give The Wrong Guy a watch. You've got a ton of people with impeccable comedy pedigrees on top of their game. The film doesn't have the twisted, surreal sense of humor of a Kids in the Hall sketch, but it's not going for that. It's not the most hilarious thing ever. It's just a good, funny movie made by a lot of Canadians.

Like, a lot.

JASON PAUL COLLUM'S SILVER JUBILEE

BY DR. RHONDA BAUGHMAN

It was nothing short of an honor to interview Jason Paul Collum for this issue. I've followed his career forever, cornered him at a convention for an adorable picture I still have stashed in my memory trunk, and honestly, his first *Femme Fatales* cover story was (what I consider) my first writer/ journalist shoutout in an industry magazine as well. I love the beauty and synchronicity of life's full circle, especially when artists are involved. To another 25, Jason!

Rhonda: Twenty-five years in the business! Congratulations! So, how do you feel about this milestone?

Jason: I'm pretty proud of what I've accomplished in 25 years. At the same time, I'm stunned that it's been that long. My first movie would have graduated from college and had its first grown-up job by now. It might have even gotten married and had a baby on the way! It seems significant to have been this length of time, which up until the last year or so, hadn't really sunk in until I decided to make a celebratory summer out of it by putting (almost) my entire library back out. Suddenly, I'm not the young filmmaking kid. I'm not a parent, but I feel in some sense like I've moved into that role for younger filmmakers. I seem to be getting asked questions of new indie kids as though I'm the dad. It's strange but appreciated.

Rhonda: Did you think, 25 years ago, this is what 25 years into the industry's future would look like?

Jason: No. At some point many years ago, I started to realize that the style of B-movies of my generation was no longer important to everyday teenagers. Then, in the last five years or so, I feel like movies in general aren't as important. Teens can't (a) hold their attention to a film for a 90-minute feature and (b) are far more entertained by 90-second videos on TikTok, Snapchat, et al. Lately I've been wondering

how much of a place there is for me in this business. It's no shock that physical media is going away and streaming services like Amazon don't like us. We're pests. When the Amazon accountants have to send me a payment for $50 (or less) for one of my titles, I'm sure it's an annoyance. Most of my filmmaking kin have been having their titles pulled by Amazon for years because of their "quality." J.R. Bookwalter has been hit several times and warned me it was coming. Somehow, I made it under the radar until just a few weeks ago when they pulled *5 Dark Souls* (1996). I mean, it's a cheap SOV movie, so I'm not surprised that way, but it was still making them money. I also had a major struggle getting *Screaming in High Heels* (2011) uploaded. Amazon kept fighting me on it, giving me ridiculous reasons why they wanted things blurred or changed—and it wasn't the nudity! This is a movie that was licensed to NBCUniversal and aired on SyFy and Chiller for two years! So, I suspect I'm on their radar now and they just want me to go away. There has never been a ton of money at my end of the business

anyway. Ever. I make movies because I love them, and I'm happy when my investors get their money back. So, I'm struggling to figure out how I justify making my type of B-movies if there's not enough of an audience to see/pay for them.

Rhonda: Looking back, what do you see as some of the biggest obstacles to helping you achieve your goals?

Jason: I've always wanted to make B-movies, but I honestly thought I'd get to the level of a David DeCoteau or Fred Olen Ray, who can survive on it and get work in some form of the venue. They may both be making Lifetime Christmas movies now, but they're working. My biggest struggle has been to get paid. The amount of dishonesty and distributor theft in this business is stunning. The worst example is *Screaming in High Heels*. I actually had an agent—Jamie Thompson of Lighthouse Pictures— who had made some really lucrative deals for some of my colleagues. He made the deal with NBC and Breaking Glass. NBC paid him immediately, but he never paid me my share. Breaking

Glass has made $40k on that title, and to date, has paid me $279. Likewise, I was always treated and paid fairly by Tempe, but they went through a distributor—Ventura—who would get titles into box stores. *October Moon* (2005) earned back its entire budget the day it was released. So, both Bookwalter [head of Tempe] and I are waiting for that fat check to come in—and then Ventura declared bankruptcy. Almost all of it gone. Similar story with *October Moon 2: November Son* (2008). Ariztical was screwing up the sales, and I made an agreement with them to get a payout and get the title back, but they only ever paid 25 percent of that agreement. So, I then need to justify to a new investor to trust me with their money when I'm looking for funding.

Rhonda: That is positively brutal. Whom do you now know to be the serendipitous hands that allowed you to realize your dreams?

Jason: Well, I've always known them to be Brinke Stevens, who brought me into the business; David DeCoteau, who gave me my first Hollywood film jobs; and J.R. Bookwalter, who saw the talent in me and gave me that first true shot at being a screenwriter/director by producing *Something to Scream About* (2004). I also have to give *big* thank-yous to Tony Timpone and Michael Gingold at *Fangoria* for being the first magazine to print my letters and promote my films. In my head, that made me legitimate—even for a SOV, or "shitteo," like *Mark of the Devil 666* (1995). Plus, the late Fred Clarke

of *Femme Fatales* magazine[1], who accepted my first piece of journalism and made it a cover story. Can you imagine, an aspiring journalist whose very first article is given a cover story? The sense of worth that gives a kid? I wish I'd been able to tell him the significant mark that made on my life.

Rhonda: Do you have any regrets or things you wish you had done?

Jason: I sometimes second-guess what I should have done once *Femme Fatales/Cinefantastique* closed down. I moved back home to Wisconsin because I was sinking into a deep depression. I honestly had not planned to stay here. It was simply to recoup my emotions. I needed to be around family and close friends. Now, it did result in getting *Something to Scream About* and *October Moon* made and getting *Assault of the Killer B's* published. I do wonder where I'd be had I moved back to Los Angeles or tried harder to find print/editing work in Chicago. Still, I also met my husband here, and I need to be here now to help aging parents. So, in that sense, the universe worked it out.

Rhonda: I can completely relate to that answer. What are a few of those peak moments of your career— the ones you look back on and smile fondly into the sky?

Jason: Again, holding that first *Femme Fatales* cover story on my *Slumber Party Massacre* retrospective was incredibly proud and impactful, plus seeing *Mark of the Devil 666* listed in *Fangoria*. Watching the official

---

1 This is where Collum worked with *ExNat's* own publisher and editor, Amy Lynn Best and Mike Watt!

cut of *5 Dark Souls* back from Moore Video in my friend Julie King's living room, I was like, "Wait a second...this isn't all that bad. Maybe I really *can* do this professionally." Making my first short feature, *Dead Women Don't Wear Shoes* (1990), with 100 percent zero experience or formal film education showed me, in the most basic terms, I could make a movie. So, that's probably the most significant. Standing in the center of the Virgin Megastore in West Hollywood with racks of *Something to Scream About* on February 13, 2004, and looking at the line of fans—followed by a snazzy Bookwalter-funded dinner on Sunset Boulevard with the cast—is probably my happiest and most impressive. It's a sensation I've not really had again, although the standing ovation at the premier of *October Moon* on September 29, 2005, is probably a close second. Standing on the Shout! Factory set of *Sleepless Nights: Revisiting the Slumber Party Massacres* (2010) and seeing the casts of all three films around me...I think I floated through most of that day. And sitting in the audience next to Linnea Quigley as we watched *Screaming in High Heels* on August 18, 2011. I was both excited and terrified for her reaction. She threw her arms around me when the end credits rolled. So, you know...there have been a few....

Rhonda: Do you have any of those "I can't believe I did that" from your time in the biz?

Jason: It's more like things I can't believe I *didn't* do. My biggest regret—Julie Strain (Playboy's *Sex Court*) once offered to take me to the Playboy Mansion...and I declined! You are welcome to kick me! At the moment of the offer, I thought, "I'm driving a car with a clunky motor and a front bumper falling off. She's the only person I'll know, so I'd need to hang on her all night. Wouldn't that annoy her? I'm a nobody—I'm going to be so out of place." Re-gret. An awful decision made out of self-doubt and fear. That said, she once asked me to take some pics of her for her website while we had some downtime on a *Femme Fatales* photoshoot for the 10th-anniversary cover. She pulled out each of her boobs and I snapped the pic. Then, she pulled down her underwear and essentially spread her

Jason, Brinke, Bookwalter on the set of Something to Scream About (2004).

117

nether region with her fingers. After gathering myself from the shock, I snapped that picture and thought to myself, "The number of straight men in the world who would kill for this moment and it's completely wasted on me...."

One other incident—after an interview for *Femme Fatales* on the set of *The Backlot Murders* (2002), I was deep into the backwoods of the lot, up by the *Psycho* house. I was too impatient to wait for 45 minutes for the transit to return to take me back to the main lot, so I decided to walk down. Four a.m., almost entirely dark, and something followed me most of the way down. It took 45 minutes, and I was *terrified*. I still think it was a coyote. I hid in the *Leave It to Beaver* house for a short bit (which is just a shell of a building and is now the *American Housewife* set). Lesson learned.

Rhonda: Who are some of your favorite folks to work with?

Jason: I guess you simply have to look to my film entourage. Brinke and Judith O'Dea (*Night of the Living Dead*),

Darcey Vanderhoef (*The Frightening*), Tina Ona Paukstelis (*Aswang, or The Unearthing*), and Karen Dilloo (*Mark of the Devil 666*) are in almost all of my films. Jerod Howard, Jeff Dylan Graham, Julie King, Sy Stevens, Brian Vanderhoef (all *October Moon 1 and 2*).... Everyone I've worked with has been a true professional, even if they're not professional actors. Behind-the-scenes editor Derrick Carey (*Hole in the Wall*) has consistently made me look like I know what I'm doing. He's a *huge* B-movie junkie, so he fully "gets" the genre and what fans want to see. I've been relying on Andrew Gibbs for being my cinematographer for nearly a decade. He always knows that camera inside and out. Plus, Eric Arsnow, who has been doing my graphics and CGI going back to my one attempt at comedy with *Shy of Normal* (2011). He's responsible for that seriously freaky spider sequence in *Safe Inside* (2017). He has also been rendering all of the poster art on my films and designing the DVD/Blu-ray wraps going back to *Shy of Normal* and *Screaming in High Heels*, plus the 2012 *5 Dark*

The Original Scream Queens: Brinke Stevens, Linnea Quigley, Michelle Bauer.

Souls release. That includes the reverse-sleeve layouts/liner notes on all of my 2020 discs. *And* I need to mention J.R. Bookwalter, who has always treated me like a pesky little brother. I'm sure there are others, but like following the Oscars, I'm afraid there are others I'm leaving out.

Rhonda: Who else would you like to work with?

Jason: I made a goal to hire each of the girls from *Something to Scream About* for future projects. I still need to get Brandi Burkett (*Slumber Party Massacre 3*), Debra De Liso (*Slumber Party Massacre*), Ariauna Albright (*Witchouse 1 and 2*), Denice Duff (*Subspecies 2–5*), and Lilith Stabs (*Mega Scorpions*). Sadly, Julie Strain has been in ill-health and is no longer able to work. I will say, though, she did a lot to help me out in my *Femme Fatales* days. I think of her often. I'd also like to get Linnea, Michelle Bauer (*Hollywood Chainsaw Hookers*), Cassandra Peterson (Elvira), and Julie Brown (*Earth Girls Are Easy*) on one of my sets. And I keep threatening to get one of those *Vanderpump Rules* girls (probably Scheana Shay) in front of my camera.

Rhonda: You have some serious credits from different roles on a film set. Where do you feel you shine the brightest?

Jason: I'm at my best directing. I loved all the experiences with DeCoteau on *The Brotherhood 1* and *2*, *Final Stab* (my favorite film set experience), *Voodoo Academy*, and Bookwalter-produced films like *Mega Scorpions* and *Bad Movie Police*. Where I personally feel most in control and

getting my vision and hoping I'll have a positive effect on people is in directing a film. Writing scripts or doing journalism is fun but can be tedious. Directing a group of people and having a shared experience fills my heart...so long as I'm in charge....

Rhonda: What are you working on right now?

Jason: Presently I'm finishing getting *Jason Paul Collum's Unlucky 13* prepped for a late September 2020 release. It's a six- disc collection of *almost* my entire film catalogue. Many of those same titles have been put out on single discs for collectors. It will premiere two items never before released: *5 Dark Souls, Part III: Retribution* (2003) and a TV pilot, *Inside the Red Room* (2019). The only title not included is *Sleepless Nights* because I don't own the rights—that was work-for-hire. I just finished a 30-minute *Screaming in High Heels Reunion* with Linnea, Brinke, and Michelle Bauer, which is the first time the three ladies have shared in a conversation in almost 25 years. Finally, I'm in the midst of directing *Everything I Need to Know I Learned from the Letter People*. It's a documentary about a kindergarten educational reading program from the 1970s and '80s (still minorly in use) that had such an effect on the children who experienced it that 50 years later, those now-adults can recall intricate details about it. Name one other program from your childhood that you can retell in detail. Stressfully, COVID-19 has slowed the process down because so much travel was involved for interviews, but we'll get 'er done!

I'D BUY THAT FOR A DOLLAR!

BY MIKE HAUSHALTER

One of my favorite activities is to look through bargain bins and the racks of second-hand sellers to find movie deals. Whether it's a forgotten A-list title, a blink-and-you-missed-it indie release, or last year's hot direct-to-home-video release, as long as it costs $2 to $5, it's bound to come home with me. But if it's less than that? Well, I'm willing to take a gamble on almost anything that's priced at a dollar and offers even a tiny bit of intrigue or interest. After all, I can't even rent most of these things for that price, and if they don't work out, I can sell them again. But when they do work out, it's magical. Here's a roundup of my latest finds, good and bad.

• • • • • • • • • • • • • •

HOLLYWOOD HOMICIDE (2003)

THE BOX SAYS:

"From Oscar-nominated Ron Shelton (Best Writing, Original Screenplay, *Bull Durham*, 1989) this hot action comedy is guaranteed to keep you on the edge of your seat... and in stitches. Starring Harrison Ford and Josh Hartnett, *Hollywood Homicide* redefines the buddy-cop genre. In Hollywood, no one is who they really want to be. Veteran police detective Joe Gavilan (Ford) and his rookie partner, K.C. Calden (Hartnett), are no exception. Between Joe's struggling real-estate business and K.C.'s fledgling acting career and yoga instruction, they've got a major murder case to solve. With both Internal Affairs and their main suspect on their tails, Joe and K.C. have to infiltrate the dangerous world of the hip-hop recording industry. Juggling two careers proves to be a comical adventure, with Joe and K.C. desperate to stay alive long enough to catch their big break."

WHY I RISKED A DOLLAR:

Well, it was not because of the box cover, because that is horrid. This is one of those films that I had wanted to see but never got around to because I just kind of forgot about it. This is pretty much one of the forgotten A-list titles I speak of in the introduction.

THOUGHTS:

Hollywood Homicide is a goofy, lighthearted cops-and-robbers romp and a straightforward Hollywood popcorn flick, nothing more nor less. This is not to say there's anything wrong with popcorn flicks. In fact, I really liked it, but I am also not surprised that it's a mostly forgotten film.

PLUS:

Awesome chemistry between Ford and Hartnett. Josh Hartnett's inability to remember the names of any of the women he is sleeping with. Harrison Ford at his best. Great cast and tons of cameos, including Keith David as a police captain, Martin Landau as a fading producer, Lou Diamond Phillips as a crossdressing snitch, Smokey

Robinson as a cabbie, Robert Wagner as himself, and Eric Idle as a celebrity.

MINUS:

Brings nothing new or memorable. Very likely to be a film that you remember nothing about a week or two after you see it.

SHELF/BIN:

Looks like it's a keeper. For one thing, my wife likes it, and it also has audio commentary, which is two pluses right there. Besides that, I know I would watch it again myself.

• • • • • • • • • • • • • •

HOLLYWOODLAND (2006)

THE BOX SAYS:

"Based on the true story of Hollywood's most notorious unsolved mystery, *Hollywoodland* is a tale of glamour, scandal, and corruption in

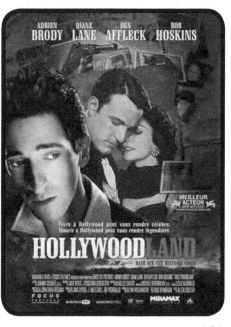

121

1950s Los Angeles. When George Reeves (Ben Affleck), star of TV's *Adventures of Superman*, is found dead in his home, millions of fans are shocked by the circumstances of his death. The police and the studio bosses want the case closed as a suicide, but rumors linger. Louis Simo (Adrien Brody), a private investigator, picks up the trail and begins to piece together the actor's last, tension-filled days. Who pulled the trigger? Was it the seductive yet scheming fiancée, the spurned lover (Diane Lane), the enraged husband (Bob Hoskins), or was it Reeves himself?"

WHY I RISKED A DOLLAR:

Hollywoodland had a lot of press when it came out, but I still somehow missed it and never got around to seeing it on video either. I came across it at an Exchange a few weeks after finding *Hollywood Homicide* and thought it would be a good time to give it a look-see.

THOUGHTS:

This is an almost-great film that has some moments of brilliance, but overall, I found the film to be rather unsatisfying. My biggest gripe about this blatant bit of Oscar bait is Adrien Brody; he doesn't ever convince me that he is a character living in the late '50s. He takes up space that could have been better filled by more time spent on Ben Affleck's take on George Reeves. In fact, I would have much rather seen a full-blown biopic about Reeves, starring Affleck, than this mess of a mystery. For my money, you are better off tracking down Reeves's episode of *Unsolved Mysteries* than giving this any of your time.

PLUS:

Great costumes and details that really capture the time period in which the film is set. Affleck is an awesome TV Clark Kent/Superman. Great performance from Diane Lane.

MINUS:

Frustrating ambiguous ending. Fails both as a mystery and a biopic. Affleck doesn't get enough time to fully explore his role as Reeves. Extraneous characters. Bob Hoskins is kind of a letdown.

SHELF/BIN:

I knew about halfway through that this was going to be a one-and-done film. It's just not a film I am ever going to want to revisit.

• • • • • • • • • • • • • •

THE LOSERS (2010)

THE BOX SAYS:

"An explosive action tale of betrayal and revenge, *The Losers* centers on an elite Special Forces unit sent to the Bolivian jungle on a search-and-destroy mission. But the team—Clay, Jensen, Roque, Pooch, and Cougar—soon finds that it has become the target of a deadly double-cross instigated by a powerful enemy known only as Max. Making good use of the fact they are now presumed dead, the group members go deep undercover in a dangerous plot to clear their names and even the score with Max. They are joined by the mysterious Aisha, a beautiful operative with her own agenda, who is more than capable of scoring a few points of her own. If they can take

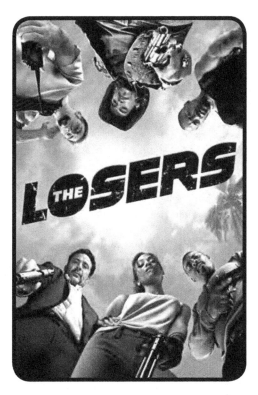

down Max and save the world at the same time, it'll be a win-win for the team now known as the Losers."

WHY I RISKED A DOLLAR:
I saw *The Losers* at the movies when it came out and seemed to remember that I kind of liked it. A dollar for a Blu-ray seemed a good way to find out if my memory served me right.

THOUGHTS:
Turns out I was right: I do kind of like it. I like it quite a bit in fact. It's a super-fun, action-packed comic book adventure with great characters, lots of snappy zingers, and a boo-hiss villain you just can't wait to see get his just desserts.

SHELF/BIN:
This one's a keeper and has a place between *The Long Kiss Goodnight* and *Lord of Illusions*.

. . . .

DOLLMAN (1991)

THE BOX SAYS:
"Brick Bardo (Tim Thomerson) is a traveler from outer space who is forced to land on Earth. Though regular-sized on his home planet, he is doll-sized here on Earth, as are the enemy forces who have landed as well. While Brick enlists the help of an impoverished girl and her son, the bad guys enlist the help of a local gang. When word leaks out as to Brick's location, all hell breaks loose.

Brick is besieged by an onslaught of curious kids, angry gang members, and his own doll-sized enemies, and he must protect the family who has helped him and get off the planet alive."

WHY I RISKED A DOLLAR:

It's *Dollman*! Wouldn't you buy a Tim Thomerson movie for a dollar, or almost any Full Moon movie for that matter? Besides that, I had not seen *Dollman* since the laser disc era, and I had it, *Bad Channels*, *Seed People*, and a few other Full Moon films in my collection.

THOUGHTS:

This is a really fun, low-budget guilty pleasure B-movie from Albert Pyun and Charles Band's Full Moon Pictures. It's a fast, funny film that strives for nothing but pure entertainment. As I mentioned, I had not seen this in decades, and I forgot how fun this film is.

PLUS:

Tim Thomerson is fantastic as tough-as-nails Dirty Harry clone Brick Bardo. Good early work from Jackie Earle Haley (*Watchmen*). Great cheeky dialogue. Lots of blood, guts, and ultraviolence. Flying head villain. Dollman's sidearm, the "Groger Blaster" (a .475 Wildey Magnum)— the most powerful handgun in the universe! Short running time. Did I mention how great Thomerson is?

MINUS:

Some wonky special effects. Shows its threadbare budget in some places. Weak/sometimes ludicrous script. Underwhelming ending.

SHELF/BIN:

We got ourselves another keeper here, folks. Be sure to check out *Bad Channels* and *Dollman vs. Demonic Toys* for more Dollman action.

•   •   •   •   •   •   •   •   •

SHARK WEEK (2012)

THE BOX SAYS:

"A group of complete strangers find themselves isolated by a wealthy madman on his island compound. They are forced into a horrifying gauntlet where they must survive a barrage of ever-deadlier species of shark."

WHY I RISKED A DOLLAR:
I am a sucker for killer-shark films, and The Asylum has made quite a few good ones. The movie also has a really great cover, and they would never slap a good cover on a bad movie, would they?

THOUGHTS:
Unfortunately, The Asylum has made quite a few horrible shark films as well, and quite frankly, this is one of them. In fact, it's one of the worst. It's so bad that it made me angry. It has a few moments of off-kilter brilliance that could have elevated it to cult status if the special effects had been done with the least bit of competence. But mostly, they took the concept of *Jaws* meets *Saw*, threw it into a dumpster, and then set fire to it.

PLUS:
Yancy Butler's killer legs. Also, she really oozes sex, violence, and menace in a way I have not seen before. Great-looking stock footage. Nice oceanside location. Land mines. Patrick Bergin is freaking amazing as the film's villain, Tiburon, a megalomaniac out for revenge. He chews up more scenery than the sharks chew up his hapless victims. Bergin seems to be

channeling all of his angst and anger into his part in this low-budget chum to the point that it's kind of scary and far beyond the scope of the film.

MINUS:
Dreadful CGI, and I mean that with all of my heart. Toothless sharks. Editing is a mess. The script stinks. The rest of the cast cannot compete with Butler and Bergin and, in fact, don't even seem to be trying.

SHELF/BIN:
After a lot of thought and weighing both the pros and cons, I decided to chuck this film into the chum bucket.

125

Exploitation Nation—Premiere Issue! We kick off with everyone's favorite sub-genre: the **Lesbian Vampire Film**. In this premiere issue, Dyanne Thorne interview; "lost" interviews with Clive Barker and his *Saint Sinner* stars, Mary Mara, Rebecca Harrell. Plus reviews! $5.99

#2: Cryptids of the Cinema: Bigfoot, Nessie, The Mothman, The Yeti, The Pope Lick Monster - we got 'em all! Well, most. The monsters and the movies that love them. Also this issue, journalist Mike Watt takes a look back at his time covering 2009's *Sorority Row*. Plus, bidding a fond farewell to **George A. Romero**. $7.99

#3: Bizarro Films. Contributions from Heather Drain and John Skipp. PLUS: Jose Mojica Marins, aka "Coffin Joe"; an interviews with filmmakers Rolfe Kanefsky; Greg DeLiso and Peter Litvin, and EXCLUSIVE INTERVIEW with Stephen Sayadian (aka "Rinse Dream"). $7.99

#4: Rock 'n Roll Movies! 144-pages! Interviews with Paul Bunnell (*The Ghastly Love of Johnny X*); Jon-Mikl Thor and Frank Dietz (*Rock 'n Roll Nightmare*); *Slade in Flame*; AIP's *Beach Party* films; Prince on Film; goodbye to Harlan Ellison; Richard Elfman on *Forbidden Zone*. $7.99

#5: Alternate Reality Warning: not a single title in this book is real. Interviewee Larry Blamire ("The Lost Skeleton Cadavra") is real, but the interview isn't. Plus: The Beatles' adapt *Lord Of The Rings*, directed by Stanley Kubrick; David Lynch directs *Revenge of the Jedi*; Amos Poe's remake of *Alphaville* with Debbie Harry; the film adaptation *A Field Guide To Film Gods*. ALL HAIL CINEMAGOG! $7.99

#6: Underground Comix! Did your old man throw YOURS away? Interviews with: Stephen Bissette, Trina Robbins, Mike Diana, Frank Henenlotter, Greg Ketter, Mark Bode, Howard Cruse's final interview; plus Buddy Giovinazzo, Vaughn Bode's final essay, *Confessions Of A Cartoon Gooroo*.

Note: #6 Boasts two covers, sold separately: $7.99 each

#7: Indie Filmmaking issue! * Mark Savage and his new film *Purgatory Road*; James L. Edwards and *Her Name Was Christa*; Gabe Bartalos and his newest, *Saint Bernard*; Scooter McCrae and his adventures with the British censorship; Carmine Capobianco (*Psychos in Love*); Henrique Couto (*Babysitter Massacre*); Revjen Miller (*The Adventures of Electra Elf*). $7.99

#8: Witnesses for the Defense! Our writers to defend a movie only they seem to like. From *Grease 2* to *Ernest Goes to Jail* to *Godzilla '98*. PLUS an **exclusive interview with director Terry Gilliam** and *The Man Who Killed Don Quixote*! $7.99

#9: When Nature (and Elder Gods) Attack! Cover by interviewee **Tom Sullivan** (*Evil Dead*)! PLUS a tribute to Stuart Gordon; Lovecraft movies; Tippi Hedren tries to kill her family in *Roar!*, Asian Worm Horror! And much more! $7.99

Grindhouse Purgatory #15: In this special issue, we say goodbye to our friend, actor, and mentor, Sid Haig. His friends and fans come from all over contribute remembrances of this amazing man and his incredible career. From his early days starring in Jack Hill's exploitation epics, to his resurgence in *Jackie Brown* and *House of 1,000 Corpses*, Sid was a unique performer and a lovely person. $9.99

Night of the Living Dead '90: The Version You've Never Seen by Tom Savini. Take a look at the intended version of Tom Savini's remake of *Night of the Living Dead 1990*, thorugh this unique book collecting the full storyboards for this film for the first time. Thirty years after the fact, the true story can be told. With annotations by the director and exclusive photographs! This is a unique look at a classic film. $29.99

Shadows & Light: Journeys With Outlaws in Revolutionary Hollywood by Gary Kent. Writer, director, actor, stuntman, special effects guru, production manager Gary Kent tells his Hollywood story, chronicling his adventures with Brian De Palma, Bruce Campbell, Ed Wood, Charles Manson, Frank Zappa, the Hells Angels and others. This is the first printing from Happy Cloud Media, LLC, with an updated Afterword. $19.99

A Whole Bag of Crazy: Sordid Tales of Hookers, Weed, and Grindhouse Movies by Pete Chiarella. Hustler, pot fiend, porn expert.take a walk down a dark alley with 42nd Street Pete as he recounts his tales growing up on "The Deuce". Criminal activity, classic undesirable cinema, pot, booze, pros, cons. The '70s: uncut, uncensored. If you really remember the '70s, you were lucky to have survived them. $14.99

Movie Outlaw: The Prequel by Mike Watt is a revamped republishing of what was previously-known as *Fervid Filmmaking*. Featuring essays on 70 underseen films including *Keep Off My Grass, Dr. Caligari, Forbidden Zone, Coonskin, Head, Psychos in Love,* and many more. A rare interview with director Stephen Sayadian. 350 pages. $15.99

Movie Outlaw by Mike Watt. Essays focusing on more than 70 underseen films including Johnny Depp's directorial debut, *The Brave*; *Don's Plum*; Mauritzio Nichetti's *Volere Volare*; *The Ghastly Love of Johnny X*, the last 35mm black 'n white science fictional musical ever made! 472 pages. $19.99

Movie Outlaw Rides Again! By Mike Watt. Essays on 70 underseen films: *Crazy Moon*; *Frankenhooker*; *Jane White is Sick and Twisted*; *The Magic Christian, Meet the Feebles*; *Impure Thoughts*; *The Stunt Man*; *Night Breed*; Brian DePalma's *Phantom of the Paradise*, Will Vinton's *The Adventures of Mark Twain*; *The Redsin Tower*. 392 pages. $19.99

Son of the Return of Movie Outlaw by Mike Watt. Essays include: *Accion Mutante;* Ralph Bakshi's *Heavy Traffic*; *Down and Dirty Duck*; *The Thief and the Cobbler*; *The Sinful Dwarf*; *Performance*; *Muppets Most Wanted*; *Legend of Simon Conjurer*; *Sorority Babes in the Slimeball Bowl-O-Rama*; *Shock Treatment*; *Yellowbeard*. Interviews with Jon Voight and Ralph Bakshi! 352 pages. $19.99

Hot Splices by Mike Watt. Eight interwoven tales about the Film Addicts, the Cinephages who devour film for the high, the bleeding perforations in their skin is just part of the game. There are five forbidden films that can induce madness or release the Dark Gods that created them, speaking through the psychopathic director. Fiction. $14.99

Order today at www.happycloudpublishing.com!

Made in the USA
Monee, IL
26 October 2020